DIFFICULTIES IN MENTAL PRAYER

❀

A New Edition
of a Classic Guide to Meditation

M. Eugene Boylan, O.C.R.

Foreword by Michael Casey, O.C.S.O.

Christian Classics   *Notre Dame, Indiana*

Cum permissu superiorum
Nihil Obstat: Patricius Dargan,
    Censor Theol. Deput.
Imprimi Potest: ✠Ioannes Carolus,
    Archiep. Dublinen.,
    Hiberna Primas.
17 February 1944

First Published 1943.

Founded in 1865, Ave Maria Press is a ministry of the Indiana Province of Holy Cross.

www.christian-classics.com

ISBN-10 0-87061-254-9 ISBN-13 978-0-87061-254-1

Cover image © AgnusImages.com

Cover design by John R. Carson.

Text design by Katherine Robinson Coleman.

Printed and bound in the United States of America.

Library of Congress Cataloging-in-Publication Data

Boylan, Eugene, 1904-1964.

  Difficulties in mental prayer : a new edition of a classic guide to meditation / M. Eugene Boylan ; foreword by Michael Casey.

    p. cm.

  ISBN-13: 978-0-87061-254-1 (pbk.)

  ISBN-10: 0-87061-254-9 (pbk.)

  1. Meditation--Christianity. I. Title.

BV4813.B65 2010

248.3--dc22

                                    2010035573

❀

To Mary

The Mother of Christ

Who Gave Her to Us

for Our Own

CONTENTS

❁

FOREWORD

Fr. Eugene Boylan's book *Difficulties in Mental Prayer* was first published in 1943 and has gone through many printings since then. It was received with great enthusiasm because readers recognized that the author was a practical man who was familiar with the real challenges that people encounter in the life of prayer, and who had good suggestions to help his readers to make progress. Fr. Eugene's insistence on the importance of confidence in God and in the merits of Christ was good news for many, liberating them from the common scourges of scrupulosity and excessive concentration on their own shortcomings, and inviting them to find refreshment in the consideration of God's mercy.

The difficulties to which the title refers often derived from following too doggedly the prevailing method of prayer termed, in those days, "discursive meditation." Although such systematic meditation may have been useful for some, especially beginners, many found its ongoing practice unnecessarily dry and unyielding. This difficulty may have been due to an intuitive temperament, to the particular situation in which people found themselves or, commonly, to the progress they had made in the ways of prayer.

Fr. Eugene preferred the more ancient approach, which recommended a simpler and more affective prayer during prescribed periods, plus a steady practice of spiritual reading or *lectio divina*. He appreciated the importance of a sound theological understanding, but considered this as an ideal to be pursued parallel to the practice of prayer. For him, prayer was a time to cultivate a personal relationship with Christ, and to allow this relationship to develop naturally, becoming ever more suffused by love as simple prayer begins to move towards contemplation.

In line with the monastic tradition in which he was formed, Fr. Eugene also insists that progress in prayer is dependent on goodness of life: "Prayer will not develop unless the soul is advancing towards the fourfold purity of conscience, of heart, of mind, and of action." Fr. Eugene was known as a sympathetic confessor and once said that he would be glad to have as his epitaph: "This man welcomes sinners," but he understood well that there needs to be a harmony between prayer and life.

Difficulties in Mental Prayer was acclaimed when it first appeared because it spoke to the specific needs of the pre-conciliar period. This was a time in which religious and seminarians were bound by rule to fixed periods of "mental prayer" and diocesan priests were strongly encouraged to make similar allowances in their daily schedules. This meant that whether or not they felt so inclined, a solid slab of time was allocated for prayer on a daily basis. And so, difficulties arose. Today, when prayer regimens are more loosely controlled, those who find difficulty in prayer often shorten it or abandon it altogether—and in this way the difficulties arising from daily practice do not have a chance to make themselves known. Fr. Eugene was aware of this danger. It is clear to him that, whatever the difficulties encountered by someone trying to pray, those caused by not praying are greater. As he notes, for one "whose heart is not in his search for union with God, life is a perpetual misery."

Times have certainly changed in the intervening years since this book was written, and the reader will quickly become aware that there have also been changes in the language and style of spiritual writing. Notwithstanding this, the outstanding content of this book is so theologically solid and practically helpful, that contemporary readers will find much in it to help them to discover for themselves creative solutions to their own particular difficulties in mental prayer, and much more besides.

Michael Casey, O.C.S.O.
Tarrawarra Abbey, Australia

BIOGRAPHICAL
INTRODUCTION

❀

Early Years—Education

Richard Kevin Boylan was born on February 3, 1904, in Bray, County Wicklow, twelve miles south of Dublin. His youth was spent in Derry, Northern Ireland, where his father was a bank manager. He had two brothers, Stephen and Gerard, and two sisters, Moyra and Kathleen. All but Gerard would one day be religious. For his secondary schooling, Kevin—as he was known then (later Eugene in religious life and the name I will use henceforth)—attended the famous O'Connell School in Dublin run by the Christian Brothers. His father, Richard, was a graduate of the school. During the school term, Eugene lived with his uncle in Dublin and spent holidays at home in Derry.

Eugene used "R.K." for a signature and was known as "Orky" in his later school years and at the university. He did not particularly like the nickname.

His mother, Agnes Colclough-Boylan, was musically gifted as would be her children. Local priests often gathered at the Boylan house for an evening of music with Mrs. Boylan at the piano. Thus, Eugene grew up in a family atmosphere where priests frequented the house, and where music and cultural interests played a considerable part in the family's own entertainment and leisure activities.

After his father retired and the family moved to Dublin, Mrs. Boylan taught music and singing, mainly plainsong, in the schools. Well-known in musical circles, she also had a great love for theater, herself being a flamboyant personality. There is no doubt that Eugene took after her in this regard. He always spoke warmly and affectionately of his mother and readily expressed his admiration of her. He especially enjoyed telling stories in which she figured as causing surprise or astonishment to passersby. Eugene's father was a quiet, devout man whom Eugene would later refer to as the "Saint Joseph of our house."

University

Eugene entered the archdiocesan seminary at Clonliffe College, Dublin. From there he attended University College Dublin, as was the custom for all students for the priesthood. His brother Stephen, two years older than Eugene, was studying for the priesthood as well. After two years in the seminary, Eugene decided that the diocesan priesthood was not for him. He left the seminary, but continued at University College to study science.

Eugene excelled in the sciences and maths. He was keen on debating and joined the university's debate club. Here he honed his natural flair for public speaking. With his excellent voice and the foundation laid in the debate club, he developed a powerful and commanding delivery which served him well throughout his life.

Coming from a musical family, Eugene played the piano with flair, was a very fine singer, and had a first-class ear for music. He enjoyed sports as well, particularly swimming. He competed in national swimming events and developed the barrel chest of a powerful swimmer. His gait was slightly awkward; he tended to roll in his walk.

Eugene was remembered by contemporaries as pleasant and easygoing. He was attentive to the uncertainty and shyness of students who were only just beginning their time at the university. One student remembers Eugene writing "NBG" on a piece of faulty equipment. When the student took this for some arcane scientific reference and asked what it meant ("no bloody good"), Eugene laughed and told him he would have to learn that mathematical formula quickly or else be in trouble. Eugene excelled in his studies. Upon graduation he earned a Rockefeller traveling scholarship which enabled him to study abroad for two years. He elected to study in Vienna.

Vienna

The city of Vienna had emerged from the First World War intact, but with the Austro-Hungarian Empire gone. While slowly adjusting to the changes in its fortunes and history, it still held much of the magic of the old Vienna in the pre-1914 years. For Eugene, fresh from the insularity of Ireland, and the smallness of Dublin, it was a place of wonder.

Eugene was in a world capital, one of the most cultured cities of Europe, and he made full use of it. He regularly attended the opera and the great orchestral concerts. However, like all students, he was often short of cash, so he and a friend would buy one score between them and follow the music from it. Despite their being banned by law, duels still took place occasionally between members of the student fraternities. Eugene recalled some of his adventures in this area, acting as second on one occasion to a former cavalry officer who left his opponent, a fraternity bully, neatly pinstriped with saber cuts from neck to waist. (Perhaps some of the stories grew with the years.) The beer cellars, the heurigen (wine taverns) with their new wines, skiing and mountain climbing, the fellowship of a large international student body—all delighted him.

A small detail that emerged during his time in Vienna was his genuine phobia about snakes. One evening, he and his friend from Dublin stopped at a fashionable shoe shop to admire the window display with snakeskin shoes grouped around two large stuffed snakes. As soon as Eugene saw these, he took off in terror and did not stop until he was a block away. When his friend caught up with him, Eugene was shaking and unable to speak—the mere sight of the snakes having such an effect on him.

More important than the cultural attractions of Vienna was the intellectual stimulation of working with professors leading the world in the fields of science and mathematics. It has been asserted by some that Eugene was associated with the beginnings of the Atomic Age by working with Ernest Rutherford (1871–1937) on atomic fission. No evidence supports this. Eugene's published papers were about atmospheric ionization rather than anything to do with atomic fission.

Returning to Dublin, Eugene took up a lectureship at University College and quickly settled into the academic life. Had he remained there, he most likely would have become a department head.

Change of Direction

For several years Eugene yearned for something more than secular life could give him. He was a member of the "conventional" Catholic societies—the Sodality and the Vincent de Paul Society—but there was something more which he was seeking. Eugene had a Jesuit spiritual director who recommended that he go to Mount Saint Joseph Abbey in Roscrea to test a possible vocation to the Cistercian life. It should be noted that Stephen had entered the Carthusians at St. Hugh's Charterhouse in England, and Moyra was a nun in the order of Marie Reparatrix. In 1932, Kathleen would join the Cistercians (Trappistines) at Glencairn, Ireland.[1] His family's support for the religious vocation had an effect on Eugene. In addition, the Irish society at the time was markedly Catholic in its outlook and ethos. Devotionalism and a strong moral sense marked the Irish Church.

Eugene entered the abbey at Roscrea on September 8, 1931, and received the novice habit on October 11. He had come to the monastery with excellent recommendations from all sides—a brilliant and gifted young university lecturer, well-traveled, and the son of a devout and well-known family. He also was manifestly renouncing a promising academic career.

The novice master at Roscrea was Father Malachy Brasil, who later became abbot of Mount Saint Bernard in England.[2] Although Father Malachy was at Roscrea only during the time of Eugene's novitiate, his moderation and kindness inspired the young man. Eugene often quoted Father Malachy up to the end of his life. In addition to his duties as novice master, Father Malachy was prior of the monastery. His assistant, Father Camillus Claffey (later abbot of Roscrea) had more to do with the novices on a day-to-day basis than the novice master himself. It is probably true that Father Camillus never understood the brilliant young man who had entered the monastery. Indeed, he was overawed by Eugene. As a result, Father Camillus tended to be defensive in his relations with him. Still, Eugene had a great and lasting veneration for the older monks, and his admiration for them had fueled the fires of his own resolve and perseverance.

After two years in the novitiate, Eugene professed simple monastic vows and came under the care of Father Columban Mulcahy, later the abbot of Nunraw in Scotland.[3] Father Columban was strict (somewhat military in his exercise of authority) and totally devoted to the monastic ideal. Father Columban and Father Malachy both positively influenced Eugene. In them, he found kindred spirits to whom he could talk and unburden himself.

Eugene professed solemn monastic vows on October 15, 1936. At that time, all choir monks were destined for ordination to the priesthood. Brother Eugene took eagerly to study. He read widely and avidly, even reading the entire *Summa Theologica* of Saint Thomas. He always held that this spoke to him as nothing else in his studies.

Eugene was appointed to teach in the secondary school attached to the monastery. Scarcely a success in the classroom—Eugene was more of a University lecturer than a teacher of teenage boys—he was still popular with the students. This was partly due to the tales he could tell about life in Vienna.

Eugene was ordained a priest on May 9, 1937, and appointed to teach philosophy to the young monks. Ecclesiastical studies followed a carefully planned path at that time; there was little room for originality. Eugene taught with an enthusiasm which he passed on to at least some of his students. Eventually, he was appointed to teach moral theology.

In addition to his teaching duties, Eugene was one of the confessors in the public church of the abbey. Frequent confession was the norm at the time, and four priests were regularly assigned to hear confessions. Eugene gained a reputation for kindness and understanding. His wide reading and comprehensive theological knowledge stood him in good stead. He had many requests for spiritual direction, particularly from the religious and priests in active ministry. It was from this experience that he decided to write his first book, *Difficulties in Mental Prayer*.

Teaching on Prayer

Difficulties in Mental Prayer, published in 1944, was an immediate success. Some thought the title unfortunate, but most found that it showed them how they might solve problems in their prayer lives. Endless requests came for Eugene to give retreats, but in the climate of the time, these were invariably refused. It was only much later that he would give retreats in Australia and the United States of America.

Eugene had two outstanding charisms as a spiritual director and confessor. He could meet any account of a situation or a problem with sympathy. He was non-judgmental and inspired enormous confidence in others. While right and wrong were clear in his own mind, he never condemned anyone or turned anyone away. Secondly, he could see where a course of action was leading, long before the one seeking advice. He had great common sense and brought this to bear on any problem he encountered.

In his theology classes, Eugene frequently quoted a statement of Saint Alphonsus, who said that he had never refused anyone absolution, and Eugene proposed this as the ideal for any confessor. He also firmly believed in the virtue of "keeping your mouth shut," which he often repeated as an axiom for the counselor, embellishing the phrase with suitable adjectives. Years later, shortly before leaving Australia, he gave conferences on confessional practice and spiritual direction to the priests of the monastic community at Tarrawarra. He returned to the same admonitions: do not judge people; never express surprise at anything; realize your own weakness and sinfulness, your own need of mercy; and above all, "keep your mouth shut" unless you see some positive good to be done by talking.

Eugene had read the Cistercian Fathers (mostly in Latin), but they had not really influenced his own work on prayer. He found the schemata and clearly defined divisions and distinctions of Father Adolphe Tanquerey's *The Spiritual Life* (1930) attractive, so he taught spirituality along the same lines.[4] No doubt his scientific training and mathematical mind found this approach congenial, but he always held the person—and not the method—as primary. Therefore, he was never satisfied with a mechanical or stereotyped presentation on prayer.

Now, prayer, especially from the individual's point of view, can often be very indefinite and quite unclassifiable. Further, even if there does exist a well-marked ladder of prayer for each individual, it is by no means necessary, at least as a general rule, to know on which rung one is standing. The important thing is to avoid standing still, and to keep on climbing.[5]

Eugene's writings and teachings could certainly be applied to monks and nuns living in the cloister, but one wonders if it could really be classified as monastic spirituality. There are two main reasons for this. First, Eugene was writing for priests and active religious. They were the ones who consulted him and sought his spiritual direction, thus *Difficulties in Mental Prayer* was written. The articles he wrote for religious magazines and reviews catered to a similar audience. Eugene would eventually write two books especially for priests: *The Spiritual Life of the Priest* (1949) and *The Priest's Way to God* (1963). Secondly, the spirituality of the Irish Cistercian monasteries in the 1940s was pervaded by the Sulpician spirituality of the nineteenth century. This spirituality was geared toward the formation of priests and contained strict observances and regulations (such as self-abnegation and silence) also found in Cistercian-Trappist monasteries.[6] Eugene was influenced by this French school and frequently quoted Cardinal Pierre de Bérulle (1575–1629) and Father Charles de Condren (1588–1641) in his conferences.[7] Writers such as Dom Columba Marmion and Odo Casel were only beginning to influence the spiritual life of the cloister.[8]

Critics of *Difficulties in Mental Prayer* were severe on Eugene for patronizing the diocesan clergy. Such criticism was misplaced. Eugene was trying to encourage all priests to take prayer seriously and consider themselves called to the highest states of prayer. His book was used in novitiates and seminaries not only in Ireland but throughout the English-speaking world. It was translated into the main European languages and went through several editions. *Difficulties in Mental Prayer* established Eugene as a spiritual teacher of the first rank, and, in the opinion of some, was his best book. While he used the writings of the great masters of the tradition, he rarely quotes them in the book. Rather, he made their teaching his own. He most often quoted the New Testament—his two favorite writers being Saint Paul and Saint John. The commentaries he used most for Saint Paul was *The Theology of Saint Paul* by Fernand Prat, S.J. (1857–1938) and *The Whole Christ* by Emile Mersch, S.J. (1890–1940).[9]

Eugene's approach to Scripture was that of his period. He was writing at the time when Pope Pius XII's encyclical *Divino Afflante Spiritu* (On the Promotion of Biblical Studies, 1942) was making an impact. For Eugene, the Gospels were the vivid retelling of what it was like to know Jesus Christ, but it was in Saint Paul's epistles where

he found two central ideas that he used in his talks and writings—
the all-sufficiency of Christ, and the Church as Christ's Body.

Eugene frequently spoke in his conferences to the Roscrea community on how Christ alone was the glory of the Father. If we would please God, it must be through our entering into Christ and putting on Christ. In his later years, he cultivated the habit of ending sermons and conferences with, "Through Him, with Him, in Him, in the unity of the Holy Spirit, is all the glory of the Father."[10] He emphasized the repeated word "Him," so that it came out as a ringing affirmation of a profound theological truth. This was all the more effective in those days of the Latin Mass when the phrase was not heard as frequently as it is today. (On the other hand, it could become rather tiresome after awhile, and when listening to his conferences one sometimes wondered when it was going to be said!)

A subject to which he applied this truth was the Divine Office. He spoke of how the Office is the prayer of Christ. He had read Saint Augustine's *Ennerationes* on the Psalms and loved to quote the saint saying that when the Church prays, the one voice of Christ is heard throughout the world.[11] He considered the Breviary as the prayer of the Church and central to the spirituality of the priest.[12] Eugene would, for example, defend a priest who turned immediately to his Breviary after saying Mass. He held that this often showed a humility and an awareness of the profound meaning of the "prayer of Christ."

This Tremendous Lover

This Tremendous Lover was published in 1946. It was his summa of spirituality. One of the first quotations in the book is from Saint Augustine: "There shall be one Christ, loving himself."[13] Eugene used this statement repeatedly in his sermons and conferences to sum up the culmination of the life of faith. As the Christian "puts on Christ" he becomes one with him, and so Augustine's vision is realized. This could be called the major theme of the book.[14]

Australia

Roscrea Abbey founded the Monastery of Sancta Maria at Nunraw, Scotland, in 1946. With the monks at Roscrea still numerous, consideration was given to founding a monastery in Australia. One of the monks, Father Ignatius Keneally, had worked as a priest for some years in the goldfields of Kalgoorlie and often urged the community to begin a foundation in his beloved Australia. He was in touch with Archbishop Mannix of Melbourne who favored the project as well. However, the uncertainty of the international situation, so soon after World War II, made emigration into Australia difficult.

In June 1952, Cardinal Gilroy of Sydney visited Roscrea Abbey and urged the community to proceed with plans for a foundation in Australia. Dom Camillus sent Eugene to Australia to look for potential sites. Eugene arrived in Sydney on September 15, 1953. He was unsuccessful in locating property in the hinterland of Sydney, so he went south to Melbourne where Archbishop Mannix welcomed him. Finally, Eugene found property at Tarrawarra, Yarra Glenn (thirty miles north of Melbourne). Dom Camillus came to verify the suitability of the property, and subsequently, one thousand acres were purchased for the monastery which would be called at the time Notre Dame (today Tarrawarra Abbey).

Father Cronin Sherry was appointed superior of the new monastery; Eugene was procurator. Perhaps Eugene felt disappointed at not being appointed superior, but it did not seem so to the other members of the foundation. The superior would be in office for a few years and then there would be an election for the first abbot. If the community wanted him then, they could elect him. Also, it was hardly to be expected that Dom Camillus would have appointed him superior. Eugene was not a man with whom he would be totally sympathetic.

Eugene had reveled in the job of searching for the site of the foundation. He had given lectures and conferences to priests and religious in the eastern Australian dioceses. He could talk grandly of acquiring property, of borrowing large sums of money, of doing this and achieving that. He had deadlines to meet and appointments with government ministers and members of the hierarchy to keep. This was the life he loved. In addition, he was in at the very beginning of a great and historic venture—the foundation of the first Cistercian community in Australia.[15]

The main group arrived in Melbourne at the end of September, 1954.[16] They were met by Eugene, along with Dom Camillus and two other Roscrea monks who had flown out ahead of them. The house at Tarrawarra was not ready for occupation, so they lived for several weeks in a house owned by the Sisters of Charity.

Shortly after the founding monks arrived, an incident took place which was typical of Eugene. A group of monks was standing one evening talking to Dom Camillus when a car, a Jaguar sports model, roared in the driveway, and the driver, clearly not expecting to meet anyone, swerved quickly around them and disappeared behind the house. Moments later, Eugene emerged humming nonchalantly. Dom Camillus looked at him and asked, a little uncertainly, if that was a new car, as he had not seen it before. Eugene replied breezily that it was not new. It was second hand, a bargain, had only cost so much, and really its purchase was a matter of saving money and so forth. In the end no one quite knew why he had bought it or what it had cost. The real reason, however, was that it is much more exciting to drive a Jaguar than a half-ton pickup truck, which was what was needed. This fascination with cars and speed stayed with Eugene until the end of his life.

No sooner had the main party arrived in Australia than Dom Camillus announced that the abbot general, Dom Gabriel Sortais, had appointed Eugene as superior ad nutum for the monastery on Caldey Island in Wales.[17] The community there was in some difficulty and needed strong leadership to bring about both economic stability and unity within the community. Eugene would be superior of the monastery for an indefinite period until the community was in a position to elect an abbot. Eugene could not leave Tarrawarra immediately since he was committed to speak at the first Australian National Liturgical Congress in January, 1955.[18]

The diocesan clergy expressed their best wishes to Eugene. He was very much a "man's man" and well liked by the many priests who had gotten to know him. His monastic community, too, was losing a well-known figure who did much in establishing the Cistercians in Australia.

Caldey Island

Caldey Island, about three miles by one mile in extent, is situated off the Welsh Coast in the Bristol Channel. It had been a monastic settlement since early Christian times. In the last century, the island had been the place of the re-foundation of the monastic life, under the leadership of Father Aelred Carlyle, in the Church of England. In March 1913, the majority of this Anglican community was received into the Roman Catholic Church. Eventually, they found that the economics of life on an offshore island was too difficult, so they left in October 1928 and resettled at Prinknash, near Gloucestershire.[19]

The Holy See asked the Cistercians to take over the island in order that it might remain a monastic settlement. In response, the community of the Abbey of Scourmont in Belgium established a Cistercian monastery on the island in 1929.[20] The community remained firmly Belgian until after World War II. It was a bit awkward for young Englishmen joining a monastery located in their native land to find a lifestyle more European than English. The reading in the refectory, for example, was in French. In addition to this tension between nationalities was the economics of a monastery located on an island. The superior since 1946 was Father Albert Derzelle.[21] In September 1954, Father Albert, exhausted mentally and physically, tendered his resignation. Eugene was subsequently appointed superior ad nutum.[22] His mandate, although never spelled out, was to anglicize the community and make it economically viable.

Many of Eugene's friends wondered how he would fare now that he had a house of his own to govern. The verdict must be that he was not entirely successful. He failed to have himself accepted by the Belgians in the community, although some of the other monks liked him very much, finding him congenial and helpful. To some extent this was true of Eugene wherever he went—people either loved him or found him "hard to take." Perhaps this is the case with any strong personality.

When Eugene was appointed superior, the economy of Caldey was parlous. Living on an island required the transportation to and from the mainland of every item to be sold or purchased. The cost of living was high. Transport charges limited the profits of farm produce. The greatest opportunity for developing a self-sufficient community (financial stability) came from tourism, especially during the summer months.

An attempt was made to come up with a product made by the monks that could be sold to visitors. In 1953, two years prior to the arrival of Eugene, a perfume made from lavender and other flowers growing wild on the island was sold for the first time. With the help of a Polish pharmacist and perfumer, Henry Kobus, hand lotion made from natural ingredients as well as other perfumes were added to the monastery's products. Eugene was friendly with one of the leading Irish couture designers who publicized the perfumes and lotion. The perfume enterprise made headlines. Shops for Caldey products, which now included soaps and cosmetic items, were opened in the resort town of Saundersfoot and in London. Both shops have since been closed, but the perfume industry at Caldey continues as a small part of monastic income.

Even with the demands of his position as superior, Eugene spoke at universities and Catholic meetings. There was no shortage of invitations, and he enjoyed speaking before groups. These speaking engagements publicized Caldey, but whether it brought postulants to the monastery is less certain.

Eugene had been superior of the monastery on Caldey Island for four years. His greatest contribution, apart from the guidance he gave to individuals in their vocation and spiritual lives, was assisting the community in finding an identity for itself. By 1959, the community had become financially self-supporting for the first time. With this economic stability and an adequate number of solemn professed monks, Caldey was promoted to the status of an abbey and preparations were made for an abbatial election.

Eugene emphasized to the community the necessity of electing someone from within their ranks, preferably an Englishman. Eugene, of course, was not permitted to vote since he was a monk of Roscrea Abbey. The community did as he suggested when they elected thirty-eight-year-old Father James Wicksteed.[23] Shortly after the election, Eugene returned to Roscrea. Did he expect to be elected as abbot of Caldey? It is likely that he did, despite his exhortations to the community. He never referred to the election in Caldey as a disappointment, but several in the community were convinced that he anticipated being elected as the community's first abbot.[24]

When Eugene left Wales to return to Ireland, he left many friends behind. Volunteers, men and women, had spent summers during his time at Caldey working for the monastery—staffing the souvenir shops and serving in the guesthouse and tea rooms. His friends remained loyal to him. Even when they criticized him, they did so with affection and admiration.

Returning to Roscrea after the years in Tarrawarra and Caldey, Eugene settled into the work in the confessional, and giving retreats. He enjoyed both, but it was the retreat work for which he became popular. It was not easy for the abbot of Roscrea Abbey to continue refusing requests for retreats by Eugene. Diocesan priests and religious in the United States invited Eugene to give retreats and conferences. His retreats were inspirational and his books, especially *This Tremendous Lover* and *Difficulties in Mental Prayer*, grew in popularity.

Abbot of Roscrea Abbey

Dom Camillus Claffey, in his eighteenth year as abbot of Roscrea Abbey, tendered his resignation in 1962.[25] Eugene, fifty-eight years old, was elected as Roscrea's fourth abbot by a narrow majority on July 11, 1962. He received the abbatial blessing on August 5. The community looked forward to having Eugene as their abbot for at least ten years, but less than eighteen months later he would be dead. Many felt that Eugene did not have an adequate opportunity to achieve anything significant or to leave his mark. Eugene did, however, make a notable contribution to the community. He continued to offer monks spiritual guidance through his conferences, and he was ready to allow people the freedom he preached.

Shortly before he died, Eugene expressed to one of the monks his disappointment at how little impact he had made on the community. He expected that by virtue of his teaching, which was certainly of the first order, people would change. Communities are probably the same the world over—a net full of mixed fish as in the Gospel. Some monks are eager and enthusiastic, others less so. It was naïve of him to think that in a little over a year he would have changed people much. He believed in the goodness of people. If they were given the lead through his preaching and teaching, he thought an early harvest would result. This did not happen. The monks remained much as they were and life went on.

What then was his legacy at Roscrea? His entry in 1931 opened up the monastery to a wider world than it had known up to then. In the early 1930s, the community was introverted and knew little of life outside Ireland, or indeed of life outside the political categories of the time. Not only did the politics of the Civil War (1922) still dominate, but the idea that there was a completely different way of looking at things had not made much headway.[26] Whether the monks came from Dublin or the rural areas, the struggle for national independence, in which some of them had taken part, characterized their thinking. The Irish Church outside the monastery had little impact on it. Moreover, as a strict Trappist community, they had little to do with what they sincerely regarded as dangerous and alien to themselves—"the world." That mold was broken by this man with university credentials and a wealth of experience in the world. The very fact that Eugene persevered and professed solemn vows in 1936, in itself, opened the community to wider horizons.

Eugene's second contribution to Roscrea, and to the countless others who came to him seeking help and direction, was to break away from the legalistic spirituality of the time and lead people into a new freedom. The spirituality of the monks (as of the then Church) was one of merit, of observance, and of law, and thus rather minimalist. That it sanctified many cannot be doubted, but that it was the fullness of the Gospel of Jesus Christ as the Redeemer cannot be asserted without qualification either.

Into this climate of duty and legalism came Eugene Boylan with his incisive mind, his eagerness for knowledge, and his voracious appetite for reading. He quickly saw that it was in the New Testament—particularly in Saint Paul's epistles—that one could find a true Christian spirituality, and he went straight to that. He also read widely in the history of spirituality. Pourrat's four volume *Christian Spirituality*, which even today remains an influential work, delighted him.[27] From it, he went to the Fathers, notably Saint Augustine and Saint Thomas, and eventually to the best available commentaries on Saint Paul. With such reading it was impossible that he would not come to see the weakness of the current spirituality, and without criticizing it, go beyond it to what he was to call over and over again "partnership with Christ."

> The whole plan of our spiritual life is a loving union and intimate partnership with Jesus in which we return Him love for love. We can picture that union in three ways: as the life of Christ in us; as our life in Christ; or as what we might call a "shoulder-to-shoulder" partnership with Jesus, a constant companionship of two lovers sharing every thought and every deed.

Each of these pictures corresponds to a true aspect of the reality, the intimacy of which is so extraordinary that it defies description.[28]

Thus, he changed the spirituality of many and led them from the half-light of a feared and fearful God to the splendors of the Risen Christ.

A third aspect of Eugene's legacy is that he definitely "opened the windows" of Roscrea to admit change. No doubt some were not ready for this. Formed in the over-regulated regime of the 1930s and '40s, they found the liberty of the 1960s beyond them—and unacceptable. This is true, but it is equally true that change had to come. It came best from a man who believed in it totally himself, rather than someone who gave way only reluctantly to the pressures of the time. Eugene, however, believed in freedom and felt that if he gave people responsibility they would act responsibly.

It may be asked how Eugene would have dealt with changes that came in the wake of the Second Vatican Council. He would probably have resisted some of them, for he was conservative in many ways. For example, he repeatedly opposed the unification of choir monks and lay brothers in the Cistercian Order when this was proposed in the early 1960s. He felt this would be a mistake, and that it would exclude a certain type of vocation from monasteries. He was convinced that in Ireland, at least, there were men who wanted a simple form of life and who would feel excluded if they had an intellectual sort of formation in the monastery (This view would still attract some support today.) It is doubtful, however, if he was really in touch with the rapid secularization of Irish society. Moreover, free secondary education for all in Ireland became effective only after this time.[29]

To the end, Eugene retained a somewhat idealized notion of monastic life and community. There existed in him, alongside the remarkable gift he had for understanding other people and being in sympathy with them, the difficulty which a city-dweller has in understanding the countryman. Eugene tended to think that if the facts were set before people, they would react to them in much the same way as he himself did. Nothing could have been further from the truth.

It might also be noted that after he became abbot, his restless intellect sought outlets it did not find. Feeling that the day-to-day trivia of the office was tiresome and boring, he undoubtedly had a restless nervous energy for which he did not always find outlets in monastic life. (He would try to work off his frustrations by going out and chopping wood!)

Death

It was December, 1963. Traditionally, on the day the College of Roscrea closed for the Christmas holidays, the parents of the boys attended the school play. The abbot was expected to make a speech and greet the parents afterwards. Eugene had been up early that morning and busy all day. After the play, he entertained a group of distinguished guests at dinner in the guesthouse and then got ready to drive to Sligo, about a three-hour drive from Roscrea. He was to attend the funeral the next day, in County Donegal, of Bishop William MacNeely, the bishop of Raphoe, who had died on December 11. Normally he would not have gone so far to a funeral, but it was a special occasion since the late bishop had been a priest in Derry when Eugene was a boy and had been a family friend. Eugene felt an obligation to attend.

I was the last one to speak to him before he left. The guests had departed, and we stood on the front steps of the guesthouse. I suggested that since he had had a long day, he should go to bed and start early in the morning. He replied that by going to Sligo he would have three quarters of the journey over and would make it easily to the cathedral the next morning without having to start too early.

I further suggested he should bring someone with him, either to drive or just to help keep him awake by talking. With a characteristic gesture he put his arm around my shoulder and said, "Don't worry about me, son; I'll be all right." It was the last time I saw him alive.

It can scarcely be doubted that Eugene fell asleep driving. The car left the road on a long straight stretch and went nose first into a deep ditch. Eugene was thrown out of the car through the passenger door and lay seriously injured on the ground. It was not until a passing motorist saw the rear lights of the car shining toward the sky that help came. Eugene was rushed to a hospital where he died three weeks later. A seven-inch tear in the pericardium (the membrane surrounding the heart) went unnoticed by the medical staff because the tight strapping around his seven broken ribs prevented bleeding into the heart cavity. When the strapping was removed on January 5, 1964, Eugene died from a heart attack. His death came as a shock. The Roscrea community had been told that he was making a good recovery. The fact was that he had very little chance of survival.

Assessment

Eugene had started an autobiography, which still survives among his papers. It covers only a few years of his youth, but contains nothing of particular significance. In contrast, he wrote an article in 1961 on Cistercian spirituality for the Dublin-based Dominican magazine *Doctrine and Life*. He expounded his views on the monastic vocation and was, in his own indiscreet way, quite self-revelatory. Eugene's article was a part of a series called "Paths to Holiness." Having often heard him speak in community conferences of the temptation of what he called "careerism" for the monk, I have no doubt that this article distills Eugene's most exact thoughts on what it meant to him to be a Cistercian.[30]

Eugene begins by describing the regulated life which the monk lived at the time. He continues with what he says is most essential— for the monk to realize that he is seeking God.

> Nothing less will do. His aim is neither perfection, nor the service of God, nor any lesser good. . . . It takes the young monk a long time to see this truth . . . its realization only comes at the end of a long process when the monk realizes that the monastic life is organized to give God not so much the monk's service as the monk's own self. (287)

What God does for the monk, Eugene continues, is infinitely more important than what the monk does for God.

> In his early days, the young monk tends to seek what might be called a monastic career. His outlook is like that of a soldier, determined to achieve distinction in his country's service. (287)

Eugene points out that stories from the lives of saints encourage a notion of "achieving" great deeds for the Church. For the common, ordinary religious monk or nun, he cautions, this "achieving," even though it may be a genuine quest for holiness, can be tinged with self-seeking. He notes that many people regard holiness as they regard, perhaps, one's giftedness in music or painting. One has a natural aptitude for it, and one must work at that.

> But the holiness to which we are called is something that does not correspond to any natural disposition we may have . . . it is a participation in the holiness of Christ, who sanctifies us by communicating to us a share in his own holiness. (288)

This idea of the centrality of Christ and our coming to God only through identification with him is emphasized by Dom Eugene. It took him a long time to learn it.

> Early in his life the monk begins to see the spiritual life as a partnership with Jesus, and if he is willing to make the sacrifices such a partnership involves, he will soon find that Our Lord is generous in manifesting his love and interest in return. (288)

This, too, ends, and the monk enters the desert. Eugene uses the image of the Exodus, which he considered "illustrates and typifies very closely the behavior of the monk at this stage."

> The monk feels that God has led him out into the desert and in some way has abandoned him. He can no longer pray as he used to . . . The monastic life tends to become a monotonous treadmill without meaning or purpose . . . compared with what he could do for souls outside, his present life seems fruitless. For a time perhaps he tries to escape into intellectual studies or into some other interesting occupation. Even if he finds satisfaction in them, it is short-lived. The limitations of his library and the lack of intellectual contact put an early limit to any development in this field, and the general limitations and obligations of the monastic life frustrate most of his efforts to achieve success in any other direction. Providence seems to have abandoned him; in some mysterious way, difficulties with superiors arise; his health begins to cause added difficulties, and temptations may renew their attractive promise of an escape from the very displeasing contemplation of himself. For, frequently the monk is his own cross. He is faced with one of the greatest mortifications in the spiritual life—the complete acceptance of himself as he is, even as he has made himself. This becomes harder as his own limitations and insufficiency become more and more apparent. He begins to cry out with Saint Paul—"Who will deliver me from this body of death?" (Rom 7:24). (289)

What is the answer?

> Some day, when the time is ripe, and when he has been fully
> cured of his tendency to put his own name on all that God does
> for him, he hears the voice of the Lord: "My grace is sufficient
> for you" (2 Cor 12:9). (289)

The message may not be clear at first, he notes, and it may take
a long time to be understood. But when it is finally grasped, the
monk turns to God and says that he will glory in his infirmities so
that the power of Christ may dwell in him. This is "The Promised
Land." Eugene then links this with Saint Benedict's Rule.

> The monk is no longer called to live himself, but Christ lives in
> him . . . his very prayer is the prayer of Christ, and his claims
> on the Father are those of the Beloved Son. By emptying him-
> self and laying hold of Christ through doing the will of God in
> humility and love, the monk reaches his vocation which is to
> love God with the love the Holy Spirit pours into his heart and
> to live so that Christ lives in him. (290)

It is worth noting that Eugene ends this article with the formula "through Christ, and with Christ, and in Christ, is all the glory of
God."

Through his reading of the New Testament, Eugene Boylan
had broken out of the ascetical/achievement-based spirituality of
the time. He had come to an understanding of the true asceticism
that is self-acceptance and total poverty in the presence of God. He
had come to understand the true meaning of "putting on Christ"—
only when we shed selfishness does the power of Christ come into
our lives. This, he said, is the work of a lifetime.[31] It had been the
pattern of his own life. He had found intellectual satisfaction in
study, but that period had ended with the publication of his books.
He had been working desultorily at a book on the Mother of God
for a long time, but it may be doubted whether it would have been
completed. He had neither the intellectual stimulation nor the
library facilities for producing a magisterial work. Yet, this is what
he was aiming at, as he considered much of the writing about the
Blessed Virgin to be second-rate.

Eugene went to Australia to start a new foundation and was
brought back by the abbot general to serve as superior to the community at Caldey Island. The harvest he helped sow in Australia

would be reaped by others. It was the same in Caldey—he was not elected, and it can scarcely be doubted that this was a serious blow to his self-esteem, despite his protestations to the contrary.

Eugene returned to Roscrea, and as he wrote this article for *Doctrine and Life*, he must have been trying to come to terms with all this. In one sense, there was little achievement in his life. To anyone who is seriously seeking God in a life of prayer, books published or people helped do not add up to achievement, as he realizes that others could do the same and do it better. This is in no way to belittle either the work itself or its importance. What we are talking about is the way it appears to the person doing it, in any assessment of his own life.

Even when he was elected abbot of Roscrea, he found his impact on the community was less than he had hoped. At age 60, he probably died somewhat a disappointed man. This indicates a certain unreality in him, but it was always there. If one could meet him as an equal, one was "in." If not, then, to some extent, one felt left outside. It is doubtful if anyone got really close to him; he often felt isolated in the community. His tendency was to dominate a relationship, something of which I believe he was unaware.

Any shadows, however, should not be over-emphasized. He was as happy a person as the next. He integrated all that happened to him into an intense spiritual life, but still faced the "ups and downs" of life like the rest of humankind. Eugene was, to use the timeworn phrase, "a man before his time." He helped an enormous number of people , and he did, in fact, change the community in which he lived. He retained to the end a sort of boyishness—shown by his delight in fast cars, in visiting his old university whenever he got the chance, and in the fondness of his recollections of Vienna. There, he had walked in Arcady, and he never forgot it.

Eugene's legacy endures in a Christ-centered spirituality, in freedom of spirit, and in his approach to the life of prayer. He saw these as central not only to the life of the monk, but to anyone seeking God.

> Now the whole of God's will has only one purpose, to re-establish all things in Christ. Therefore, if our wills are conformed to the will of God, the whole of our history, with every single thing that happens to us, is part of a plan—a plan which is being carried out by the omnipotent power of God—to unite us to Christ and sanctify us in Him.[32]

Certainly, whether Eugene realized it or not, what Saint Paul talks about—counting everything as naught when compared with Christ—had happened in his own life.[33] Despite the disappointments, in the one place where it mattered his achievement had been great. Perhaps the best conclusion to this account of him is what he wrote himself in the article that appeared in *Doctrine and Faith*:

> In retrospect the long weary road seems but a short passage . . . in actual fact it was much longer, much more difficult and even dangerous. But it had its brighter moments. When most needed, God came to the aid of his servant to encourage him and strengthen him. Looking back one sees that God did everything, and was always at work, even when he seemed furthest away. Looking back one sees that the most absolute need is total confidence in the infinite goodness of God . . . for he has said "He who believes in me though he die, shall live" . . . and we have all received of his fullness, for he is given to us that nothing may be wanting to us in any grace . . . everything is simplified, everything is peaceful, everything is organized, everything leads to Christ. His (the monk's) own nothingness, his own poverty, his own powerlessness is his joy—for so Christ may be all. (290–291)

Fr. Nivard Kinsella, O.C.S.O.
Monk of Mount Saint Joseph Abbey
Roscrea, County Tipperary, Ireland

Notes

1. Father Stephen Boylan was born on October 25, 1906, ordained a diocesan priest on May 18, 1930, professed solemn vows on August 9, 1935, at St. Hugh's Charterhouse at Parkminster, England, and died on April 6, 1987.

    Moyra Boylan joined the order of Marie Reparatrix. Her name in the order was Sister Mary of St. Fintan. She made her vows on February 1, 1931 and died in Cincinnati, Ohio, on April 15, 1967.

    Kathleen Josephine Boylan was born in 1909. She entered the Cistercian monastery of Glencairn [Ireland] on September 8, 1932. Her religious name was Sister Mary Magdalen. She professed solemn monastic vows on February 3, 1938, and died on January 2, 1982, in her fiftieth year as a Cistercian. "I lived with Sr. Magdalen for twenty years here in Glencairn. She loved music [and] was very careful in her work. She was sacristan when I was a young nun, and I remember her absolutely gorgeous flower arrangement for the sanctuary on big feasts. She was honest and truthful and a very humble person in the nicest way. She had Parkinson's disease for some years before her death, but she was very independent and insisted on continuing to fend for herself as much as possible." Sister Veronica Gertrude Kelly, Glencairn Abbey, "Sister Magdalen," June 28, 2006, personal e-mail (June 29, 2006).

The youngest member of the Boylan family, Gerard, married and died in Dublin.

2. Dom Malachy Thomas Brasil was born in 1883 and entered Roscrea Abbey in 1905. He was elected abbot of Mount Saint Bernard in 1933 and served until 1959. He spent his last years at Sancta Maria Abbey (Nunraw, Scotland), the daughterhouse of Mount Saint Joseph (Roscrea) where his former novice, Dom Columban Mulcahy, was abbot. Dom Malachy died on July 28, 1965, and is buried at Nunraw. Dom Malachy attributed his love for the contemplative way of life to a retreat given at Roscrea Abbey by Dom Columba Marmion at the beginning of 1914.

3. Dom Columban Mulcahy, born in 1901, entered Roscrea in 1924 at age twenty-three. In 1948, he was elected the first abbot of Sancta Maria Abbey in Nunraw, Scotland, founded by Mount Saint Joseph (Roscrea) in 1946. He died on July 15, 1971, several weeks after a cerebral hemorrhage. He played a key role in the ecumenical movement in Scotland between 1961 and 1966.

4. *The Spiritual Life: A Treatise on Ascetical and Mystical Theology*, 2nd ed. and trans. Herman Branderis (Desclée, Belgium: Society of Saint John the Evangelist, 1930; Westminster, MD: Newman, 1947). "This work [*The Spiritual Life*], which has been translated into English, is a mine of information on every part of the spiritual life, and should be in the library of every religious house, even of those who have not been trained in theology. It is the outstanding work of reference in the spiritual life." Eugene Boylan, *Difficulties in Mental Prayer* (Westminster, MD: Newman, 1946), p. 75.

   Father Adolphe Tanquerey (1854–1932), a French Sulpician, was a celebrated scholar who wrote on dogmatic, moral, and ascetic theology. His work in dogmatic theology is presented in a two-volume *Manual of Dogmatic Theology* (New York: Desclee, 1959).

5. Boylan, *Difficulties in Mental Prayer* (Westminster, MD: Newman, 1946), p. xiii.

6. In 1642, Jean-Jacques Olier (1608–1657), a disciple of Cardinal Pierre de Bérulle, founded the Society of St. Sulpice, dedicated to the education of priests. This religious association was responsible for the establishment of

DIFFICULTIES IN MENTAL PRAYER

seminaries in France, Canada, and the United States. "Sulpician spirituality" became the norm for the spiritual formation of seminarians prior to Vatican II.

7.   "Let us note that the doctrine of our association with the mysteries of Christ's life is used as the foundation for the teaching of one of the finest schools of spirituality we have: that, namely, which is founded in the writing of Bérulle, Condren, Father Olier, and Saint John Eudes." Eugene Boylan, *The Mystical Body* (Westminster, MD: Newman, 1948), p. 62.

    These words should be balanced with comments made by Dom Eugene in a talk to religious sisters of the Society of the Sacred Heart of Jesus in 1960: "Even that wonderful school of spirituality that is associated with St. John Eudes, M. Olier, Conderon, Bérulle is contaminated with a hatred of the flesh, of the human person as consisting of a soul locked up in a vile body. Heresy! And it makes the Incarnation inexplicable. A human person consists of a body and a soul, and our bodies are just as much part of our person as our soul is. Both have to be sanctified and both are holy." Sisters of the Society of the Sacred Heart of Jesus, mimeographed transcription of talks by Dom Eugene Boylan at Duchesne College of the Sacred Heart and convent, Omaha, Nebraska, March 24–27, 1960, talk 4, p. 1. Hereafter cited as "Boylan, talk to Sisters" followed by the talk number, page number.

8.   Blessed Columba Marmion, (1858–1923) was beatified on September 3, 2000, by Pope John Paul II. He was a prolific writer on spirituality. His famous trilogy is *Christ in His Mysteries* (1919), *Christ the Ideal of the Monk* (1922), and *Christ the Life of the Soul* (1932).

    Odo Casel (1886–1948) was a Benedictine monk of the Abbey of Maria Laach in Germany, near Bonn. He developed mystical theology in *The Mystery of Christian Worship* (1932).

9.   Fernand Prat, S.J., *The Theology of Saint Paul,* trans. John L. Stoddard, 11th French ed., 2 vols., (Westminster, MD: Newman, 1956). Also by Prat: *Jesus Christ: His Life, His Teaching, and His Work* (Milwaukee: Bruce Pub. Co., 1950).

    Emile Mersch, S.J., *The Whole Christ,* trans. John R. Kelly, S.J., 2nd French ed., Religion and Culture Series (Milwaukee: Bruce, 1938). The first French edition was published in 1933. Also by Mersch: *The Theology of the Mystical Body* (St. Louis: Herder, 1951).

10. In four of his books—*Difficulties in Mental Prayer, The Mystical Body, The Spiritual Life of the Priest,* and *This Tremendous Lover*—Boylan concludes with the doxology.

11. Saint Augustine's commentary on Psalm 54 and 85.

12. "Now the Divine Office is an entering into the prayer of Christ; it is a putting-on of the prayer of Christ; it is an identification with the prayer of Christ; it is an abiding in the Vine. Therefore, when the priest opens his Breviary, he 'enters into' the prayer of Christ in a much more real way than a monk, coming into choir where the office is being sung, 'enters-in' to the prayer of the community. It is the prayer of Christ that the priest is praying. Christ is praying in him; he is praying in Christ. He is praying in the name of Christ and in the name of each of His members." Eugene Boylan, The Spiritual Life of the Priest (Westminster, MD: Newman, 1949), p. 38. Dom Eugene is writing to priests, but his words can be applied to all Christians devoted to the Divine Office.

13. In Latin: *Et erit unus Christus seipsum amans.* Saint Augustine, Homily 10 on the Epistle of St. John (1 John 5:1–3) in The Works of St. Augustine, *Nicene and Post-Nicene Fathers*, vol. 7, first series, ed. Philip Schaff (1888; reprint, Peabody, MA: Hendrickson, 1995), p. 521.

14. "The whole Christian life, then, is Christ and His love. We ourselves live and love no longer, it is Christ who lives and loves in us. In us Christ loves the Father, and the Father loves Christ in us. Christ in us loves our neighbour, and in our neighbour we love Christ. Christ in the husband loves the wife, and in the wife the husband loves Christ. So also Christ in the wife loves the husband, and in the husband the wife loves Christ. Christ is our supplement, our complement, our All in fact, both in loving and being loved. 'And there shall be one Christ loving Himself.' For 'Christ is all and in all' [Lk 9:41-42]." Eugene Boylan, *This Tremendous Lover* (Westminster, MD: Newman, 1947; Notre Dame, IN: Ave Maria Press, 1964), p. 333. This and subsequent quotes from *This Tremendous Lover* are used with permission from Ave Maria Press.

15. The foundation made by the French Cistercians at Beagle Bay in Western Australia, in 1890, had not survived.

16. The formal opening of Notre Dame Abbey was December 19, 1954. On November 29, 1958, Father Kevin O'Farrell, who was novice master at Mount Saint Joseph (Roscrea), was elected the first abbot. He served until September 17, 1988.

17. As a point of interest, Dom Eugene preached a retreat to the Caldey monastic community in 1950.

18. The title of his paper at the Congress was "The Liturgy and Personal Holiness." His definition of holiness is worth quoting: "Holiness consists in receiving and making our own the holiness we derive from Christ, rather than in the mere perfecting of ourselves . . . until we are filled with

him, until nothing is wanting to us in any grace." He then went on to show how the liturgy draws us into Christ, changes our prayer pattern, and rids us of self-centered piety.

19. A history of the Benedictine monks on Caldey Island is given by Peter F. Anson, *The Benedictines of Caldey: The Story of the Anglican Benedictines of Caldey and Their Submission to the Catholic Church* (London: Catholic Book Club, 1940).

20. The Community at Scourmont Abbey voted on the Feast of Saint Benedict, March 21, in 1928 to establish a foundation on Caldey Island. The founders arrived on the island on January 2, 1929, but the official foundation date is January 6, 1929, the feast of the Epiphany. See Roscoe Howells, *Total Community: The Monks of Caldey Island* (Tenby [Great Britain]: H.G. Walters, 1975).

21. Father Albert Derzelle was prior at Chimay Abbey (Belgium) when he was appointed prior of Caldey on February 12, 1946. He subsequently was elected as prior. On September 14, 1954, he resigned due to physical and mental exhaustion. In 1957, he went to Notre Dame des Mokoto in what was then Zaire (now Democratic Republic of Congo). He was superior there from March 9, 1967, to December 31, 1981. He was then chaplain at La Clarté-Dieu, Murhesa (also in Zaire) from 1985 to 1991. He died on April 11, 1993, at La Clarté-Dieu, where he is buried.

22. Until Dom Eugene arrived at Caldey in February 1955, Dom Godefroid Bélorgey filled in as superior. A Frenchman, Dom Godefroid Bélorgey entered Scourmont Abbey in Belgium at the age of thirty. He was novice master and prior before serving as auxiliary abbot of Cîteaux from 1932 to 1952. He spent two years at Caldey (1953–1955). He then was chaplain at the Trappistine monastery of Our Lady of Peace in Chimay (Belgium). He returned to Scourmont in April 1964 and died five months later on September 15. He wrote several books. *The Practice of Mental Prayer* was translated into English in 1952 (Westminster, MD: Newman Press).

23. Dom James served as abbot until March 14, 1980.

24. "The Irish monks seemed to think that Dom Eugene had not been fully appreciated. They gained the impression, however, that it had come as a relief to him not to have been chosen as Abbot. He said to some of them, 'The big problem was that my mother had bought a new hat in readiness for the occasion'—which seems to suggest that he took it in the right spirit. And this indeed is the truth of the matter because he was undeniably very disappointed, but demonstrated that, if he did have some shortcomings, he was a 'big' man." Roscoe Howells, *Total Community: The Monks of Caldey Island*, p. 171.

25. Dom Camillus was elected abbot of Mount Saint Joseph (Roscrea) on September 25, 1944. His resignation was accepted on February 21, 1962. He died on July 28, 1971.

26. "The Irish Civil War (June 28, 1922–May 24, 1923) was a conflict between supporters and opponents of the Anglo-Irish Treaty of December 6, 1921, which established the Irish Free State, precursor of today's Republic of Ireland. Opponents of the Treaty objected to the fact that it retained constitutional links between the United Kingdom and Ireland, and that the six counties of Northern Ireland would not be included in the Free State. The Civil War cost the lives of more than had died in the War of Independence that preceded it. It left Irish society deeply divided and its influence in Irish politics can still be seen to this day" *Wikipedia*, "Irish Civil War," http://en.wikipedia.org/wiki/Irish_Civil_War.

27. Pierre Pourrat, S.S., *Christian Spirituality*, 4 vols. (1927; Westminster, MD: Newman, 1953).

28. Boylan, *This Tremendous Lover*, p. 310.

29. For another glimpse on how Dom Eugene might have viewed the changes brought about by Vatican II, we can turn to his 1960 talk to the sisters of the Society of the Sacred Heart of Jesus. "There is one thing you have got to do—you and I and every one of us. Every fifteen years a new generation comes into the Society [of the Sacred Heart of Jesus]. You have got to adapt yourself to them. If you do not do that, the Society will cease to go on. Do not stand too rigidly on the "spirit of our Holy Mother [foundress]" or "our Holy Father [founders]." I am quoting from the pope. I was present at two conferences of major religious superiors, one in Sydney and the other in London. We were addressed both occasions by the delegate. He said, "Now, Reverend Fathers, I am not speaking in my name. To make it clear to you I am going to read what I have to say to you. Please remember that it is the pope who is speaking to you." We were exhorted to reconsider our constitutions, our customs, and the general habit of our life, including our habit, our robes, and everything else—our practices. And not to consider so much what our Holy Father or our Holy Mother did so many hundred years ago—what they said, did, and thought. But, what they would say and think and do if they were alive today, if they had the intelligence to understand the needs of today and the courage and the virtue to adapt themselves to it. That is the Holy Father's opinion. Now, to some extent, we have to adapt ourselves to a newer generation." Boylan, talk to Sisters, 5, 7.

30. The quotations from Dom Eugene's article, "Paths to Holiness, [Part] V: The Cistercians" in the January 1961 issue of *Doctrine and Faith* are used

with permission from Dominican Publications, 42, Parnell Square, Dublin 1, www.dominicanpublications.com.

31. "Let us then take as our slogan the words of St. Paul, *'I live, now, not I, but Christ liveth in me'* (Gal 2:20). Let us try to put this into practice. It means forgetting ourselves and remembering Christ. It means giving up our own petty, narrow interests and assuming those of Christ. . . . It means that we give up the dream of making of ourselves and our lives something wonderful of our own creation, in which we can take pride; instead, we now leave it to Christ to communicate to us and to form in us a beauty that is a reflection of His own and that is of His making. It means complete abandonment to Christ, and complete self-surrender." Boylan, *The Spiritual Life of the Priest*, p. 150.

32. Boylan, *This Tremendous Lover*, p. 175.

33. Philippians 3:7.

PREFACE

There is a process used for printing pictures in colour which involves the making of separate blocks for each elementary component colour in the picture. The prints from each of these blocks are superimposed on each other, and if the relative strength of each colour is correct, the result is quite natural. If, however, any one shade is too weak, then there is a corresponding defect in the final rendering of the true colour, which might perhaps be corrected by an extra printing of the weak component.

Now, the purpose of these pages is something like that of the extra printing. It is not that the standard presentation of mental prayer is defective, but it would seem that the impression of mental prayer that many souls have received needs to be strengthened in certain "colours." That purpose explains the irregular extent of treatment which the reader will notice in these pages. The subject of methodical meditation is only outlined, as there are more than enough excellent books dealing with it in great detail. Besides, the souls for whom this book is primarily intended are those who cannot succeed with the usual methods of meditation, as well as those who once were able to meditate, but now find that it has become an impossibility to do so.

In order to fit this "extra printing" into the general picture of prayer, the whole subject is, at least, outlined; certain phases which seem to need more detailed treatment being dealt with more extensively. But there is another reason why we have insisted on including a discussion of such states of prayer as those which we have called the prayer of faith, and why we beg the reader, whatever may be his position on the ladder of prayer, to read the whole work. Whatever may be said about the general law of the development of prayer when observed and averaged among a large number of different souls, most individuals find that their path of advance is extremely twisted and shows rapid and extensive variations. It would seem therefore, that except perhaps at the very beginning, an acquaintance with the nature and technique of all the different stages of prayer is not only helpful at any stage, but even necessary at all of them.

Despite the title of this work, it is not a scientific analysis or a classified catalogue of the various difficulties that may arise in prayer, with a complete practical solution of each one appended in its proper place. Its purpose is rather to discuss the nature and ways of prayer, not with scientific objectivity, but from the point of view of the individual, looking at it as it appears to him. In this way, it is hoped to put the soul in position to deal with most of his own difficulties. Further, the primary purpose is not so much to instruct the reader as to encourage him to press on in prayer, and to induce him to seek further information from the works of more competent pens. That is why the treatment of the subject is so condensed; so much so, that it will need a second reading to extract all we have tried to say. This re-reading is all the more advisable from the fact that the earlier chapters will be more easily understood in light of those which follow.

As the point is so well treated in many other works, it is assumed that the reader is aware of the necessity of mental prayer. A Christian who does not pray is like a man who neither thinks nor wills—a mere animal in the spiritual life. The pursuit of perfection is utterly impossible without mental prayer—which, of course, may be made quite unconsciously. In fact, it may be said that if a man does not pray he cannot save his soul.

We must insist that we cannot regard the "active" life in the religious state or in the priesthood as one which precludes the soul from advancing—and advancing far—in the ways of prayer. On the contrary, the religious state, if it be truly such, should both lead a soul to progress in prayer, and be a continual help to him to do so. The essential and primary purpose of the religious life is the perfection of each individual religious; otherwise it has no right to the name. Now, the pursuit of perfection is exactly what is needed to make progress in prayer possible, while, in turn, prayer is the very best means of seeking perfection, and all the more so when it is "progressive."

The same reasoning is valid with regard to priests living in the world. Although their obligations in the matter of perfection are somewhat different, and despite the fact that the difficulties they have to face are quite considerable, nevertheless all that we say of prayer even in connection with religious, applies with no less force to their case. Even though we personally have less direct knowledge of their problems, a chapter on the prayer of priests has been inserted lest clerical readers should imagine that their hopes of progress in prayer were considered to be any less than those of religious.

Nor do we think even lay-people, by their life, are debarred from hoping for such progress in prayer as we indicate in this book. Anyone who is prepared to serve God with good-will, and devote sufficient time daily to spiritual reading and to prayer, may reasonably expect to grow in friendship with God, which is to progress in prayer. The difficulties of the laity in the interior life need more detailed treatment than can be given in this book, but they are not insuperable, and need not prevent any lay person of goodwill from trying to lead an interior life of prayer even in the world.

Further, we are quite definitely opposed to the theory that there is no state of prayer between ordinary methodical meditation and passive contemplation. As we hope will become evident from these pages, prayer seems to us to be the result of a progressive intimacy and friendship with God. If prayer cannot progress, then neither can friendship.

This point is of great practical importance, for false notions in its regard may turn a soul away from all hope of achieving union with God. In the course of what follows, we will try to show how this union can be sought and found by an ever-increasing intimacy with Jesus in prayer and in work. This leads to a view of each exercise of the religious life as a meeting-place where the religious is sure not only to find Jesus, but to be able to be united to Him. Now, this view is the best remedy for what is perhaps the state of greatest misery on earth—the misery of half-hearted service in religion, for it puts the otherwise weary and monotonous routine of the religious life in an entirely new and captivating light, offering new strength and new purpose to many souls.

It will be further found that the division of prayer into well-marked and clear-cut stages has been, to a considerable extent, avoided. Definitions, too, when given at all, are often loose and sometimes vague. This, however, is quite deliberate. There is no use in trying to be more definite or more clearly classified in our notions than is the reality of prayer itself. Prayer, especially from the individual's point of view, can often be very indefinite and quite unclassifiable. Further,

even if there does exist a well-marked ladder of prayer for each individual, it is by no means necessary, at least as a general rule, to know
on which rung one is standing. The important thing is to avoid standing still, and to keep on climbing.

The fact that the same difficulty often re-occurs at different
stages in the progress of prayer, and that the same principle finds
many applications in the course of the spiritual life, has led to a
number of repetitions in the text. In a book written to meet the
needs of individual souls, and which views its subject from different
points of view, and attempts to deal with the many misunderstand-
ings and wrong notions that can be met with, such repetition seems
justified and will, we trust, be pardoned.

No apology is made for making what can only be an imperfect
attempt at the difficult task of outlining the teaching of St. Paul on
the indwelling of the Divine Persons in the baptized soul and the
soul's incorporation in Christ. This doctrine was the foundation of
all the Apostle's teaching. It still is an unrivalled foundation for a life
of prayer, and would appear to be not only the best encouragement
for it, but also the surest ground for hope of its achievement. In particular, St. Paul himself testifies that the Holy Ghost helps the infirmity of our prayer, and many theologians see a close connection
between the operation of the gifts of the Holy Ghost and the development of prayer.

That the pursuit of prayer involves the pursuit of holiness need
cause no one any doubt as to the possibility of its achievement.
When Our Saviour rose from the dead, He had taken on Himself,
and triumphed over, every possible obstacle—in our past, in our
future, in ourselves, or in our surroundings—which might interfere
with our holiness. The agony that broke His Sacred Heart in the
garden was the thought that, after He had done and suffered so
much—far more than was ever necessary—for our holiness, we
should render His Blood useless by our cowardice and by our failure to believe in Him and to trust in Him. The greatest value that
we can set on Christ's sufferings is to believe that they can make
holy even such as we are. We must, in fact, fill up the things that are
wanting in the Resurrection of Christ in His Body—in ourselves—
by letting Him rise in us through our holiness.

If there be any grace, any good, any help in these pages, it is due
to the intercession of Mary the Mother of Christ,— it is due to the

grace of the Holy Spirit, who works in the most unworthy priest,
—it is due to the sufferings of Jesus Christ, who merited all graces for
men,—it is due to the mercy of the Father in heaven, who wills to
restore all things in Christ, in whom, in the unity of the Holy Spirit,
is all His glory. To Their Name be all honour and glory forever.

September 8, 1942
Feast of the Nativity of Our Lady
The Abbey of Mount St. Joseph Roscrea

CHAPTER ONE

INTRODUCTION

Faced with the ever-increasing difficulty of leading a holy life in contact with a world ever growing more flagrantly pagan, often urged by the more or less conscious feeling of the needs of one of the most critical moments in the history of Christianity, many souls have commenced to examine the state of their spiritual health and to seek means of spiritual advancement. The need for greater spiritual energy has led them to consider especially their prayer, for they have come to realise that prayer is the source of their spiritual strength and the centre of their spiritual life.

The result of this investigation is, in many cases, unsatisfactory and disheartening. Many find that there is something wrong with their prayer; they note a lack of progress, an ever-increasing difficulty, and even a growing distaste for that exercise. Some conclude that for them it is a mere waste of time to go on "praying" as they have been doing; others find the time given to prayer a burden that is becoming well-nigh intolerable. It is with the hope of doing something to ease such difficulties that these pages have been written. While the needs of those in religion are their principal aim, there is no reason why lay people in the world should not find help in the discussion. Even beginners may take courage if the possibilities of prayer are set before them, and once their misapprehensions of the true nature of prayer are corrected, they will attempt its regular practice with renewed determination. But it is only after some continuous attempt at regular prayer has been made that these lines fully find their intended application.

1

An exact catalogue of difficulties in prayer with a definite remedy for each is not intended; rather, it is hoped that by discussing the nature and practice of prayer, and pointing out the sources from which difficulties arise, the reader will be enabled, perhaps after some experimenting, to find a solution for his problems. Since many of the difficulties arise from mistaken notions of its nature, let us first survey briefly the development of prayer so as to fix our perspective, and then return to a more detailed discussion of its various elements and stages.

Technically speaking, prayer is an elevation of the mind and heart to God, to adore Him, to praise Him, to thank Him for His benefits, and to beg His grace and mercy. In a more restricted sense, the word is confined to the prayer of petition, that is, to the asking of seemly things from God. Chief among its effects are to make us love God more and more, to conform our wills to His, to make us truly humble, and to lead us to become more intimately united to Him. It can rightly be described as a loving conversation with God, especially if it be remembered that conversation includes listening as well as talking, and that great friends can often converse without words. When we make use of a set formula with our lips and endeavour to conform our thoughts and desires in some way to our words, we have what is usually called vocal prayer. But, of course, if it is to be a prayer at all, the mind must play some part in it. In what is called mental prayer, we endeavour to originate these thoughts and desires in ourselves by some reflection, and then to give utterance to them by words—generally words of our own—or even by that eloquent silence where the heart speaks to God and gives Him fitting praise without the noise of words. But even if we do articulate words, or vocalise these acts and desires, our prayer does not therefore cease to be mental prayer. This is a mistake that some people make, thinking that they must repress all articulate utterance or speech in mental prayer. On the contrary, if, as often is the case, lip articulation helps to make our acts more fervent or more real, it can be used. But, it is not essential. In this, as in all such matters, a holy liberty of spirit should prevail.

The "acts" which we make in prayer are called affections. The ordinary meaning of this word in English is entirely different from its connotation here. Affections in prayer are essentially acts of the will, by which it moves towards God, and elicits other acts of the different virtues, such as faith, hope, love, sorrow, humility, gratitude, or praise. In the earlier stages of the spiritual life these affections usually cannot be produced without laborious consideration and tedious effort. The things of this life, the rush of human activity, the daily experience of the senses, so throng the imagination and excite the emotions that the more abstract truths of faith and the mysteries of the nineteen-century-distant life of Our Lord have little hold on the mind. Some of the time of prayer must, therefore, be spent in reviewing these thoughts and stirring up the heart to act and to give expression to its desires. The word meditation, in its strict sense, denotes this preparatory work of reflection and consideration. This is not really prayer; it is merely a prelude to prayer. The affections and petitions form the real prayer. For this reason, the custom which applies the name Meditation to the whole exercise of mental prayer is unfortunate. While reserving the point for a fuller discussion in a later chapter, let it be said here that the word Meditation in its wider sense, as applied to the whole exercise of prayer, covers far more than the strict meaning of the word. It must include some petitions or acts, if it is to be prayer at all.

As one advances in the spiritual life, convictions are developed which are easily re-animated at the time of prayer; reading and reflection—two essential foods of the spiritual life—deepen the knowledge of Our Lord and His teaching, and make us grow in His love; the reality of the things of the spirit becomes intensified. The result is that the time necessary for preliminary consideration becomes less and less, and the affections come more easily and gradually take up the major part of the time of prayer. Such prayer is called "affective prayer." Then, just as when friendship has developed between two men, mutual understanding and community of purpose ripen, and words begin to carry a whole wealth of meaning—so, too, as intimacy with God increases and virtue advances accordingly, we may find that our affections (that is, our acts of the will and of the other virtues) need fewer and fewer words for their expression, and it may sometimes happen that we are content to kneel in silent adoration, or in mute sorrow, or in some such "affection" without using words. Thus, our prayer simplifies itself. This simplified prayer is often called the "prayer of simplicity," but even when authors agree as to the definition of the term, it would seem that they frequently apply it to quite different things. And so, to prevent misunderstanding, it seems preferable here to avoid the use of the expression. The prayer just referred to may be called the prayer of simplified affections.

In all this, of course, God's grace has been at work. Sometimes, however, in the case of a soul who is generous and humble, and who refuses to compromise and sign a treaty of peace with self-love—no matter what occasional victories that enemy may have won—it happens that God begins to play a still greater part in the soul's prayer. His action is of a new type which may at first escape notice. He works in the depths of the soul and makes little or no appeal to the imagination or to the emotions, or even to the ordinary working of the intellect. This state of prayer, which here will be called a prayer of faith—without, however, insisting too much on the exactness of the term—is a prayer of great value and most effective in uniting the soul to God. It has its own difficulties and perplexities, and may demand the exercise of much patience and resolute effort. If, however, it is persevered in with generosity and confidence in God, it leads to great graces of prayer and holiness. It would be no exaggeration to call it a short cut to sanctity.

Before leaving this chapter to consider in more detail the different phases of prayer just outlined, anticipating a future discussion of the subject, it may be said that while writers divide the spiritual life into stages corresponding to the different degrees of prayer which are characteristically found in souls in each stage, there is no sharp border-line marking the divisions, nor indeed is there any strict uniformity of type within any one degree. Sometimes, for example, especially upon occasions of great joy or sorrow, even the beginner may find himself praying in a very simplified way; while, on the other hand, the advanced soul may often have to fall back on the technique of meditation to surmount some temporary disability. In all these matters there is much misunderstanding, and as many of the difficulties in mental prayer spring from these wrong notions, the next few chapters will, first of all, give a short account of the different faculties which the soul uses in its operations, and then discuss in more detail the various phases of prayer here outlined.

CHAPTER TWO

THE POWERS
OF THE SOUL

Technically speaking, man is a rational animal. With the brute animals he shares the power of sensation and sense appetite, while in common with the angels, he has an intellect and a will. In the state of grace, he is made a participator in the Divine nature and is enriched with the power to know and love God by faith, hope, and charity. All his natural knowledge depends on the working of his five external senses. He has, however, internal senses, two of which, the imagination and the memory, concern us here. By means of these powers he can recall and reproduce the images obtained from the outer senses, by a sort of a talking picture, as it were. He can even reconstruct new pictures—or phantasms, as they are called—out of the material supplied by former experience. In addition to these powers of sense-knowledge, there is also the very important faculty of sense desire, called the "sense appetite," which desires any good or attractive object which the senses set before the subject, either in reality or in imagination. This faculty is automatic; that is, it acts immediately on the presentation of the object to it, and its action is often accompanied by what the philosophers call a passion, which produces some corporal effect. We can see this appetite—the word has a much wider application here than in ordinary speech, for it covers all movements towards the good of any sense—at work in our moments of anger, or, for example, in the desire for forbidden foods on days of abstinence. In passing, it may be noted, that since this desire is automatic and, therefore, outside the control of the will, it can never be a sin in itself. If this were clearly understood, much trouble about supposed consent to bad thoughts and to anger, and the like, would be avoided. There *is* a desire there, but only in the sense appetite; there can be no sin until the intellect recognises the sinful nature of the object, and the will desires it. Thus, on Friday morning, no matter how much such a man's "appetite" desires meat, as long as his will refuses to yield, not only does he not sin, but he can even merit considerably.

This digression, introduced because of its importance in another connection, brings to our notice the higher faculties of the intellect and the will. The intellect is the faculty by which man *knows* truth; its scope is indicated by its power of knowing abstract truths, relations, universal ideas, etc. In this life—in its natural mode of operation at any rate—it works by abstracting its knowledge from the concrete individual objects depicted in the imagination. But even after the intellect has obtained matter for thought, the imagination still keeps trying to form some image to represent the ideas with which the intellect is working. That is why abstract thought is so fatiguing, for the imagination can never fully achieve its purpose; it must often be content with picturing a word, or some vague image, to suit the idea. Its efforts can be illustrated by trying to see what "picture" we form of God. Its limitations can be illustrated if we try to picture the notion of "dependence" or of "causality" or of "honesty," or of any such abstract idea.

The will is the intellectual appetite; that power by which we desire or "love" objects which the intellect pronounces good. Everything can be regarded as good in some respect; even sin is willed as good—a good of the senses, for example. Merit belongs, ultimately, only to acts of the will, and it is through the will alone that sin can be committed. On the working of the will the whole of the spiritual life depends. The will is a free faculty, whose action is subject to ourselves in such a way that no created object can force it to act.

Because of this dual nature in man, there are a number of reactions to which he is subject, and which we shall loosely call emotions or passions. These are rooted in his sensitive, or animal, nature. The joy, with its corporal expression, which a boy finds in getting first in an examination is probably more rational than sensitive in its origin; the eagerness with which the same boy retaliates when attacked comes more from his sensitive nature than from the action of the intellect. To this latter type of reaction belong many of those "feelings" which are found at prayer: consolations, aridities, sorrow, joy, etc. That is why the subject has been introduced here, for it is obvious that, *in so far as they come from the senses,* such movements are in themselves not meritorious, nor are they even signs of true devotion, which consists in the readiness of the will to serve God. They are, however, of tremendous help in overcoming the resistance of the "flesh" to serving the spirit, and assist us to devote all our energies to the service of God. In practice, no human being could serve God with his whole heart, unless his sensitive nature found some delight to draw it to God; for we are men, not angels. But there is a tremendous difference between the "feelings" that have their origin in the higher powers and which overflow into the senses, as sometimes happens—especially in the higher flights of the spiritual life—and the "feelings" that have their origin in the senses, and which tend for their own sake to draw the higher powers down after them. Much of the "devotion" experienced in the earlier part of the spiritual life has a good measure of this latter "feeling" in it. God forbid, however, that we should despise it, for often such consolation may come from God. It is a great help to detach our hearts from the consolations of creatures, and to move the whole heart in its search for God. But to imagine that real devotion consists in such feelings is a fatal error.

There are other points of importance in this connection, but since the above is sufficient for our immediate purpose, they can be left for later treatment, and we may go on to consider the first stages in prayer.

CHAPTER THREE

DISCURSIVE PRAYER

By discursive prayer is meant a prayer in which reflection or consideration of some mystery or of some truth of faith predominates. "Discourse" was the old word used for the process of reasoning by which one came to the truth gradually—step by step, as in one of Euclid's demonstrations. The opposite action of the intellect might be called "intuition," where the mind takes in a truth at a glance, either because it is self-evident—"the whole is greater than its part," for example—or, in a less strict sense, because long experience has made one so familiar with all the steps of the argument leading up to it. All, for example, see the axioms in Euclid by intuition, while many of the propositions are so familiar to the teacher that he may now be said to see them by intuition. The term "discursive prayer" is here introduced for a deliberate reason. In the strict meaning of the word, "meditation" applies to the discourse of the mind with the accompanying workings of the imagination and the memory, and to that alone. Since, however, in many religious houses, the name meditation is given to the exercise in which a stated time of the day's programme is set apart for mental prayer, the word is often applied to any form of mental prayer. Even if a religious is raised to the heights of contemplation, he is said to be "at his meditation". This usage has its disadvantages; it takes away a very useful word, which will here be replaced by "reflection" or "consideration," and it leads those who take the name too strictly to

9

think that the essence of this exercise of mental prayer lies in the
considerations.

Now, in reality, the fact is that there is no real prayer until the
soul starts making "acts," or affections. This cannot be too often
emphasized. The purpose of consideration, reflection or "meditation" in its strict sense, is merely to lead the soul to produce acts. It
has other effects to be considered later, but once the acts come, its
work is done and it should be put aside until the soul can no longer
go on making acts—or, in other words, can no longer go on talking
to God in some way or other, for that it is in which prayer really consists. If such conversation with God is found possible at the very
beginning of the time of prayer, no attempt should be made at considerations as long as our conversation with God continues, even
though this may mean leaving considerations out altogether. (Such,
at least, is our opinion, but not all would exactly agree with it. On
this point, and on the matter of this chapter and the next, see the
Appendix.)

Since however this is not usually the case, at least in the beginning, some method of reflection will be of tremendous help. The literature on this subject is enormous, and most people are acquainted
with the common teaching to some extent at least. Numerous
authors have drawn up, and expounded and developed, in more or
less detail a "method," which in the main essentials is generally
closely related to that used by St. Ignatius in his celebrated *Spiritual
Exercises*. The subject of the meditation is prepared the evening
before, divided into "points," and the main conclusions, acts, petitions and resolutions to be arrived at, are determined. When the
time of prayer has come, the exercise is commenced by putting oneself in the presence of God; there are certain preludes to fix the faculties by a "composition of place," etc., certain preliminary
petitions; the first point is taken, and the imagination and intellect
applied to it in methodical fashion; certain acts are elicited; then the
second point, and perhaps a third, are dealt with in similar fashion.
The predetermined acts, petitions, and resolutions—together with
any others that suggest themselves during the exercise—having
been made, the prayer concludes with a "colloquy" or conversation
with God or with some of his saints, and a short thanksgiving, to
which is added an examination of the manner in which the exercise
has been performed. Some thought may be selected to be kept at

hand during the day, to renew the effects of the meditation in the soul. The whole scheme is familiar to anyone who has used one of these Manuals of Prayer, which in some cases prescribe the programme in great detail, and there is no need here to treat of it at any greater length.

When a method of this sort is followed, it certainly leads to success, and it forms a most useful way of helping the beginner in his first attempts at mental prayer. The many souls who can follow it are in no need of our remedies, but it is desirable to warn them to be ready to modify their method should it cease to be helpful, and to put them on their guard against the mistake that may be made through a wrong notion of the essential nature of prayer: of thinking that reflection is prayer, and of failing therefore to give enough time to the making of acts and talking to God. They may perhaps find new hope in the suggestion that there may be further possibilities open to them. There are many souls who have reached a high degree of holiness, and who never seem to have used or needed any other way of praying. We say "seem" because, as will appear later on, it may be that while "meditating" with the lower part of their mind, they are, all unknown to themselves, contemplating God in a special way with its highest powers. The same thing may be true even of vocal prayer, especially of the choral recitation of the Divine Office. In any case, there are many paths to holiness, and while the graces of advanced prayer are a powerful, if not the greatest, help to progress, they do not in themselves constitute holiness. If a man loves God with his whole heart and with his whole soul, and with all his mind and with all his strength, he has fulfilled all the law, and he is perfect, no matter in what way he prays.

There seems, however, to be a number of people who, despite continued efforts and undoubted goodwill, not only fail to find any help in the use of these methods of prayer, but are even hindered thereby, sometimes to such an extent that the whole business of prayer becomes an intolerable burden. As a result, that which should be the source of their spiritual life becomes dried up; perseverance becomes difficult, and advance is only achieved by heroic efforts. The soul may even give up all attempt at prayer, and end in spiritual disaster. Then, there are those who were once successful in prayer, but who found as time went on that they could no longer pray as they used to do, and were reduced to a state of complete powerlessness at meditation, not knowing any other way to pray. All such souls, it is hoped, may find the beginning of the solution of their problems in the following discussion of mental prayer. Lay folk need not be deterred by the fact that at times it is clearly the case of priests and religious that is being considered. Most of the points to be raised, and all the principles indicated, can apply to those in the world who want to lead a life of prayer and to sanctify their day's work.

CHAPTER FOUR

MODIFYING
THE METHOD

The detailed methods of discursive prayer, found in so many manuals and which are a difficulty to the class of souls we are now considering, are of comparatively recent growth; their spread dates from about the sixteenth century. In the old days, when the religious life was more monastic in form, and faith perhaps more lively, the need for such a detailed plan was not so generally felt. The notion also of mental prayer as something confined to a special short period was quite foreign to the minds of the time. To what extent private prayer was made in common by the old monks is not quite certain; such an exercise would be rather a means of stirring up the fires of prayer, so that they might burn steadily for the rest of the day, for the whole day was looked on as a time of prayer.

The work of meditation, in the sense of reflection and consideration, was supplied by spiritual reading—which was done slowly and thoughtfully—and was continued by actual reflection and by pondering over the truths of faith or the mysteries of Christ during the time of manual labour or the free periods of the day. Acts of ejaculatory prayer throughout the day helped to turn the heart continually to God, and the Divine Office gave utterance in a definite and inspired form to the feelings and the needs, not only of the individual soul, but also of the whole Church, the Body of Christ. Thus, when a religious betook himself to private prayer, the preparatory work was already done and he went straight to the actual business of praying.

In course of time, the development of the religious state brought many distracting activities into the lives of its members, and in most cases made the public recitation of the Divine Office impracticable. It was then found desirable to make a regular practice of marking off a set time for mental prayer, and to make this one of the principal exercises of the day, not in order to limit its practice, but to ensure at least a minimum of attempt. This development was probably hastened by the results of the Renaissance, which saw the decline of the medieval spirit of faith that had permeated even the lives of the laity. Nowadays, all religious houses, even those of the monastic orders, have a time set apart for mental prayer, while the Canon Law urges a similar practice for the secular clergy. To sum up the effect of this change, one might say that the whole of the monk's day had been compressed into an hour or so and fitted into the life of the modern priest or religious, in order to make sure that, for some part of the day at any rate, he should rise above his cares and pre-occupations and talk with God.

Since the object of this change is not to limit prayer but merely to insist on a minimum of it at least, it follows therefore that if, for a particular place, or for a particular person, this process of compression can be reversed and some of the old spirit partly restored so that one's prayer overflows into the other hours of the day, it will be most desirable that one should do so. For this purpose, spiritual reading, which is of so much importance in the spiritual life, could become more or less of a meditation. Spiritual reading and mental prayer are as necessary for the life of the soul as the daily food is for that of the body. Without constant spiritual reading, not only can there be no progress in prayer, but there is not even any hope of perseverance in the spiritual life. To try to lay down a minimum time for this exercise would be too delicate a matter. The grace of God can always adapt itself to circumstances, and the circumstances of each religious house are a very special part of His plan. Where there is sufficient time at an individual's disposal, however, it may be said that to reduce the time for spiritual reading, without due cause, to less than three hours in the week, is to starve the soul, and will bring about the consequences of such starvation. And it would seem that, for at least half of this time, the reading should be done personally. A total diet of public reading can hardly be sufficient to meet the needs of each individual.

In some religious houses, owing to special circumstances, it may not always be possible to spend half an hour daily, even in broken periods, at this exercise. Where that is the case, one should be careful to seize such opportunities as may occur on Sundays or holidays, or during the vacation time, to nourish the soul by suitable reading. In those houses where books are read for the community, each individual should supplement the general fare by reading in private such matter as suits his own special needs. Everyone should keep himself familiar with both the deeds and the words of Our Saviour, for they are the revelation of the Word of God. The building up of a vivid living memory of Our Lord by frequent reading is of great importance. Further, one should make oneself acquainted with the general scheme of the spiritual life, and in particular with the doctrine of prayer, even in its higher stages. This equipment is necessary in order to co-operate with the changing phases of God's action; it will also help one to make the best use of any available direction.

Once this spiritual knowledge has been acquired further reading should be done without haste, digesting and savouring what has been read, and occasionally making such acts of prayer as suggest themselves. Reading, which should never be commenced without a short, but fervent, prayer for help, should always be regarded in a spirit of faith as containing a message from God Himself somewhere in the lines read or between them, which prayer, faith, and confidence will make perceptible. This spiritual reading is the foundation— one might say, the essential foundation—of a life of prayer, and is it the best preparation for that exercise. If it is carried out faithfully, the need for long and methodic consideration at the time of prayer will be rapidly reduced; in fact, this may even become quite impossible. Consequently, the ordinary methods of mental prayer must then be modified to suit the needs of such a soul. As further progress is made in the knowledge, and more especially in the practice of, the spiritual life, not merely will the considerations be lessened, but the acts or affections will become much simpler. In fact, one particular act will gradually come to include many of the others usually prescribed in the method; moreover, the nature of the acts may so change that it is difficult to observe them, for there are many movements of a loving heart that escape human observation. Who can count the "acts" of love that a mother makes beside her sleeping child? The method of prayer will thus need further modification, and indeed at this stage methods may be put aside.

Since the purpose of consideration prescribed in the methods of mental prayer is principally to lead to acts or affections, such consideration may, and indeed should, cease as soon as the acts come. When that stage is reached where one can "pray"—that is, make acts—from the very beginning of the prayer, these considerations, apart from a few moment's recollection at the beginning to fix one's attention, may be left out of the prayer altogether. Of course, if the facility to pray ceases, one may have to fall back on consideration to make a fresh start. But one must be on guard against the mistake of thinking that considerations are an essential part of mental prayer. There is, however, another valuable fruit that comes from considerations: those strong convictions about the principles of the spiritual life, the reality of the supernatural, etc., which are developed and deepened by frequent reflection. Care must be taken to sustain these convictions when reflection is no longer used at the time of prayer. That can be done by spiritual reading, especially when made in a meditative way, or by frequent, almost unconscious, reflection during the various parts of the day. One can easily realise how a business man or a professional man is always thinking of his affairs, continually "meditating" on them: seeking improvements and devising new ways of advance. If a soul is taking its spiritual life seriously, it will be assiduous in its consideration of ways and means, in its search for truth, and in its endeavour to follow the truth when known. Thus, without deliberate determination, it will give quite a lot of thought to its spiritual life during odd moments of the day. Meditation in this sense should never be given up; for if a man thinks not in his heart, his whole spiritual life may soon be laid desolate.

The resolutions, too, which are generally indicated in the method, must not be overlooked. It may happen that they are not made during mental prayer. Then, they should be made or renewed during the examination of conscience; they will probably become much simpler and more general as time goes on. But as long as there are particular failings to be overcome, especially if they are habitual, there is need of particular resolutions to combat them. Given, then, that the soul finds that it can pray without having to reflect at length on various points, and that it provides for reflection and for the renewing of its resolutions during some other part of the day, there is no reason why methodical meditation should not be omitted in favour of a freer and fuller talk with God, at least as long as such a state of affairs continues. For, when all is said and done, meditation is only "thinking about God," while prayer is "talking to God," a conversation which may develop into "looking at God and loving Him."

CHAPTER FIVE

SOURCES OF
DIFFICULTY
IN PRAYER

Not only is it unnecessary for a soul who has made some
progress in the spiritual life, and who supplies the matter and
the convictions that lead to mental prayer by reflective spiritual
reading, to make a point-by-point meditation when he comes to the
time of prayer, but it would also be beset with difficulties. This is
especially true when one is ready for the next type of prayer, in
which reflection is reduced to a minimum and acts or affections predominate, where the whole prayer, in fact, is a loving colloquy or
conversation with God. To inflict the use of a "method" on such a
one is to try and force a sprinter to use crutches. No wonder a soul
so circumstanced finds meditation an intolerable burden! But,
before considering this next type of prayer, let us first see whether
there may not be other reasons why the use of a prescribed method
may be troublesome and may form an obstacle to success, even
though the individual is not yet at the stage of proficiency in the
spiritual life, but is still quite a newcomer.

It would seem that many authors, in considering the ascent of
the ladder of the spiritual life, begin with the condition of an habitual sinner, in whom the teachings of the faith have been more or
less neglected, and a great measure of free rein given to self-love
and to the desires of lower nature. The question may be asked

whether such a scheme, with the consequent prescriptions of matter and method for prayer, may be applied to the type of soul that
is met with, say, in Irish seminaries and novitiates. Most of the clerical students and the young men and women who enter religion
here, or who start seriously to take up the practice of the spiritual
life in the world, have already imbibed the convictions of the faith
in their very infancy, one might say, and have lived, at least in their
earlier days, in the atmosphere of the faith. It is true that they may
have been thoughtless and never have considered the real meaning
of their religion, but at least they have had sufficient conviction to
lead them to enter the seminary or the religious state, and that frequently, just after their school-days. Generally, too, habitual sin of
any serious type is rare among such subjects, and there are many
who still preserve their baptismal innocence. Surely, such a soul does
not need, nor can it face, the long, tedious plodding of a course of
"prelude and point" meditation for many years. It is true that it will
have to be educated in the spiritual life, and that the new knowledge
will have to be digested by reflection. But this is often done quite
spontaneously in spiritual reading, and hardly needs such a detailed
plan of attack as is called for in the case of one who is trying to
effect his conversion from a life of sin. To make such souls "meditate" without some modifications in the method is often to set them
building a house already completed.

Proper spiritual reading will produce the necessary conviction
with regard to the new truths that they learn, if indeed the docility
of their faith and the readiness of their fervour do not do so spontaneously. The earnest resolutions that are one of the fruits of meditation will generally arise spontaneously in affective prayer; if not,
then the examination of conscience will supply them. Therefore, it
would seem that such souls are often really ripe for some sort of
affective prayer, even though afterwards it may be necessary for
them to make use of meditation for some time. Their direction calls
for prudence, but to insist that all should adopt methodical meditation seems a mistake. It would be far more profitable to put them in
touch with the person of Our Lord, and let them become intimate
with Him in loving conversation. Such intercourse with Our Lord is
an excellent corrective for their defective habits, and will quickly
mould them according to His heart.

There is another reason that makes this policy desirable. The demands made on the time of the modern priest and religious by his work and the preparation for it, leave a minimum for the more interior exercises of the spiritual life and for the development of a life of prayer. If such a one does not get into touch with Our Lord before the full burden of intense activity is laid upon him, it is not then so easy for him to develop a type of prayer that can easily be fitted into his day's work; whereas, if he has previously had some practice of affective prayer, he can soon acquire the habit of talking to Jesus during his work. Even if after some time it becomes necessary for him to return to meditative prayer during the time set apart for that exercise, so that he may complete his spiritual formation, nevertheless, he has acquired a habit of ejaculatory prayer that is of inestimable value, and has made the first step on the way to the transformation of all his activities into true prayer.

There is another type of temperament that finds great difficulty in discursive meditation. Some minds reach their conclusions by a sort of intuition rather than by a long discourse of reasoning. When a subject is set before them, they quickly draw out of it all the fruit available at the moment, and the harvest will not be increased by prolonged consideration. It is not till later on, in the light of new knowledge and experience, that their convictions are deepened and extended. Such souls have little to gain by trying to keep the mind fixed for long on the points of a meditation. It is better for them to proceed to the acts, and try to talk to Our Lord, or if that fails, to repeat phrases of some favourite prayer, slowly and thoughtfully. This difficulty can easily arise when, as in some religious communities, the subject and the points for meditation are read the evening before and, again, in the morning during the time of prayer. At the first hearing, the mind may often—there and then—extract as much as it can from the subject-matter, and is ready to proceed to pray immediately. The repeated reading in the morning is then wearisome enough, without having to go through the matter point by point. In such cases, one should try to speak to Our Lord, or else fall back upon a new subject. It is well always to have some predetermined alternative. The fifteen mysteries of the Rosary form a programme of prayer for many souls. Others make a similar use of the Stations of the Cross. Another way is to remember that Mass is beginning somewhere at every moment. If one follows that Mass in thought and imagination, it can provide suitable matter for prayer.

Another source of difficulty in mental prayer lies in the choice of a subject. In this matter, the needs and attractions of each individual must be considered. Where the choice is left to oneself, the ordinary rules of prudence—especially if advice is sought from some competent authority—will settle the matter. But what of the case where the subject is read for a community the evening before, and repeated point by point next morning? This is a delicate question, and calls for some compromise. There are two extremes to be avoided. First of all, every religious, whatever be the needs of his soul or whatever be his progress in the ways of prayer, should ever be on his guard against despising or disdaining in any way any such spiritual food coming from authoritative sources. The provisions made by superiors are a very special part of God's Providence, and are filled with grace. Anyone who listens to such reading in a spirit of faith, saying in his heart, "Speak, Lord, for Thy servant heareth," will find that God makes special use of it to illumine and strengthen his soul. It may be only one small point—a single word, perhaps, that He uses—but it will fit into another context, that of God's other dealings with that soul, and will be a source of grace. It will be done unto us as we have believed. It is a matter of great importance that souls, especially advanced souls, should be very careful of their attitude in such circumstances.

On the other hand, it seems unreasonable to demand that every soul should make its prayer on the lines of the meditation read for the community, and to deny individuals the right to follow the attractions of grace. Avoiding these two extremes, every soul of goodwill, while preserving its liberty of spirit, should give preference in such a case to the matter so provided by those charged with its government. If this can be made use of for prayer, even if only as a starting-point for a colloquy with Our Lord, that should be done. If, however, it does not fit in with the soul's needs and with the workings of Divine grace, it may be quietly and respectfully laid aside. It often happens that among the points read out, there is a Divine reminder for the soul of the need to renew its familiarity with some special truth or the like, by reflection or by reading at some other time, without its being necessary for the soul to abandon its own way of prayer at the moment. In all this matter there is clearly need for discrimination and prudence, and it would be well if those who find it necessary to develop their prayer along individual lines should occasionally take counsel with some competent adviser, be he superior, priest, or even a prudent colleague.

Under present conditions it often happens that for many souls a suitable guide is not always at hand; but between annual retreats and the various journeys that holidays and ill-health demand, it will generally be possible to consult some "specialist" and establish relations with him. Once a competent guide has been found, to whom one can easily open one's mind, and who has been made acquainted with one's circumstances, an occasional letter will be enough to provide for all the normal uncertainties of the spiritual course. In this matter, too, God will always adapt His grace to circumstances, so that where no such guidance can be found, He will make other arrangements. But where competent advice is easily obtainable, it would be folly to reject it.

In the case under consideration, to charge with singularity or with pride everyone who does not follow the subject read out or who feels the need of a book to fix his thoughts, especially in a community which includes members of all ages and of various degrees of religious experience, seems rather arbitrary. It is impossible to expect that in such a community the same spiritual food should be suitable to each one's needs. Of course, the caprices of every individual cannot and should not be humoured. But there is need for prudent discernment and a holy liberty of spirit. However, where custom has already established a canon in these matters, religious should be prepared to accept the limitations arising either out of circumstances—such as the lack of a light—or through the direct decree of superiors. The grace of God can always adapt itself to such providential circumstances, and confident resignation to God's fatherly care will always ensure His special help. We may be quite certain that those who resign themselves in this and in other similar matters cheerfully and confidently, will progress far more quickly, and with greater solidity, than if they tried to insist on getting their own way. Be it noted that God often gives during the day, even in our most active moments, the graces that He withheld during the time of prayer. In fact, for a soul who takes care to accept and to adapt himself to all the workings of God's providence, especially when He seems to set obstacles in its path, His ways, however unreasonable they may seem at first, are in fact full of a most wonderful tenderness and merciful bounty.

CHAPTER SIX

TOWARDS
AFFECTIVE PRAYER

So far we have been considering difficulties that arise at prayer, through the use of a method which is unsuited to one's state or temperament. The general test of suitability in this connection is twofold: facility in the exercise and soundness in the result. Of the two, the second is the more reliable, and is sometimes the only sign of a proper way of praying; for if a soul is praying in the way best suited to his state, it will be manifested in the goodness and fervour of his life. One who tries to adopt a manner of praying beyond his spiritual strength or age will soon find himself involved in difficulties, and will begin to fail in regularity and to fall away from his former fervour. But if, for example, a soul finds that he can spend the time of prayer in loving intercourse with God, even though he uses few words, and if, at the same time, he does not begin to fall off in fervour in the other actions of his spiritual life, nor to develop that touchiness of pride that refuses to accept even the smallest humiliation or neglect, then he may and, indeed, should be allowed to pray in this way. This is affective prayer, which will be treated in a later chapter.

But what of the soul who is not yet ready for such prayer, and who, despite goodwill and earnest efforts, can find no help in the ordinary method of meditation? Here, since individual needs differ, it must suffice to make suggestions which may indicate a line of approach that will lead to the solution of this sort of difficulty.

Nowadays, thank God, daily Communion is a regular practice, not only in religious houses, but with many souls outside the religious state. While there are a number who use a book to make their thanksgiving, there are a great many souls who are able to persevere in prayer for the usual fifteen minutes without any such help. Indeed, many more would do so if they had not a wrong idea of the way in which Our Lord wishes to be entertained, for they think that we must use the formal terms of a prayer book instead of speaking to Him in our own incoherent words. This thanksgiving would seem to offer a way of approach to mental prayer, for, be it well understood, unless it consisted in the mere formal recitation of a long list of vocal prayers by heart, it must have been true mental prayer. Suppose, then, we begin our prayer with a spiritual communion— quite an informal one—not worrying much how we must word the invitation to Jesus to come into our hearts (for "fine speeches" should be avoided like a plague in private prayer), but paying a whole lot of attention to Him whose presence is the cause of our prayer, for He is already in our souls from the time of our baptism as long as we are in the state of grace. Then, we can proceed just as we do after Sacramental Communion. Most souls have worked out some programme for this time to suit their own needs.

The four ends for which Mass is offered, for example, might supply four headings for prayer, which could be developed in familiar conversation with Our Lord. These are: to adore God, to praise Him and thank Him for all His gifts, to atone for our sins, and to beg His grace and mercy. This colloquy, or conversation, with Our Lord could be modified to bring in the point or points which are the subject of our prayer. Very often the points of a meditation just read for us can be so used. Thus, for example, if the hidden life of Our Lord be the subject, we can talk to Our Lord about His days in Nazareth, familiarly, intimately, as a man is wont to speak to his friend. We can ask Our Lord questions about those days; we can listen to what He has to say to us about them. We can tell Him about our own day's work and compare notes with Him: "Did you find the work so tiring? Were your customers unreasonable and hard to please? Did your back pain you after the continual bending over the carpenter's bench? Didn't you know much better than St. Joseph how to make things?—You who made the whole world! How did you force yourself to spend thirty years of your short life in such a way, with the whole world waiting for your teaching and your deliverance?" etc., etc. Then we should talk to Him of our own life, of our difficulties, of our failings, of our shortcomings, of our sins. Oh, yes! especially of our sins! . . . for this Man receiveth sinners and shall save His people from their sins. The sins for which we are truly sorry can bind us to Our Saviour, and the great secret of all intercourse and close partnership with Jesus is to give Him a chance to be a Saviour to us.

If there is some particular difficulty in our life, if there is something unpleasant we have to face that very day, let us speak to Him about that. If there is something that keeps coming in as a distraction, let us turn that into a prayer by talking to Our Lord about it. Let us tell Him about the toilings that give us so much trouble in our daily work; let us tell Him of some attachment that we cannot or even do not want to break. The great way to convert distractions into prayer, and to change a bad or an imperfect will into holy determination, is to talk to Our Lord about them, just as one speaks to a friend, remembering that He is appointed by God to save us from our sins and from all that leads to sin or negligence. We must never forget that since He is God!, He is omnipotent, and therefore that there is absolutely no depth of sin or of weakness, of darkness or of despair, from which He cannot or will not deliver us. Nor may we forget the intense love that made Him deliver Himself up to the tortures of the Cross for us. Therefore, there is no one who need be afraid, no one who has not the right to draw near to Him, to talk to Him, to show Him his sins, to speak to Him of his spiritual life in any of its aspects, as one talks to a doctor about sickness, to a friend about one's affairs, or to a lover about one's life, with its sorrows and joys, its hopes and its fears.

The underlying principle in this way of acting is one that must be emphasised as of capital importance in all phases of the spiritual life. It is this: the essential point is to get into touch with Jesus as early as possible in the spiritual life, in each of its exercises, especially that of prayer, and to keep in touch with Him by all possible means and at all costs. This way of acting will remove from meditation the elements that make it distasteful and difficult to certain types of souls. It is also a remedy for a very common misunderstanding of the true nature of mental prayer, for many people have the notion that this is purely a mental exercise, a work of the intellect and its attendant faculties: to discover truth, to understand it, to form convictions, and to lead to resolutions—a work of the head, but not at all of the heart. In reality, all this is merely the prelude to prayer; it is not prayer itself.

There is another consideration to be urged in this connection. For many souls, an abstract or impersonal view of virtue, of perfection, of the joy of heaven, or of any such consideration, will generally leave the heart untouched and excite no desires. It neither produces prayer nor presses one on to the practice of virtue. Personal contact with Our Lord puts the whole spiritual life in an entirely different light and, often without much explicit consideration or particular resolutions, leads the soul unconsciously on to the practice of many virtues and puts new energy into its spiritual course. An analogous effect is seen in human affairs, where one is led and encouraged by the example of one's friends, while the capacity of a man in love to change his most characteristic ways and forget his selfishness is proverbial. This point could be developed at length—for the spiritual life is a love affair with Jesus—but space forbids. Let it suffice to say that this is a principle that will solve many, if not all, of the difficulties in the life of the soul, for Jesus is the Way, the Truth, and the Life. Even in the dry and arid stages of contemplative prayer, when the soul seems incapable of a good thought or affection, when God seems to be nothing more than a word of three letters—we can still keep in touch with Jesus. The real contact with Him is made by faith—faith in His love and mercy. We lay hold of Him by hope and we cling to Him by love, however dry our act of love may be as long as it is an act of the will accepting the will of God. But further discussion of this point must wait for a later chapter.

There is one abuse of mental prayer which it might be well to indicate here, one into which all those who teach or preach are liable to fall. It consists in making their mental prayer a preparation of the mind for work, rather than a stirring-up of the will to pray and to love. Some, too, spend the time of meditation "preaching" to themselves, being chiefly interested in finding fine thoughts and words to do so to their own satisfaction. Talking to Our Lord "in one's own words" should be a remedy for this disease. Sometimes the list of acts prescribed in the book we use is so long and so detailed that it crushes our efforts and makes the whole thing sheer drudgery. It can be taken as a guiding principle that no one should ever feel bound to exhaust all the acts on the list. If any one act is sufficient to keep us occupied, it should not be put aside on the plea of going on to the next one. As long as the heart is occupied with God, whether in speech or in silence, that is enough.

Another way in which too much attention to a method can interfere with our success at prayer is that it may have the result that all our acts become "reflex" acts. Not merely do we make an act, say, of faith, but we *watch* ourselves doing so, and that rather critically, taking notes all the time of everything we do. Apart from being no small burden, this may lead to a harmful pre-occupation with one's self instead of with God. This is the ruin of any prayer, for prayer is a pre-occupation with God, and the higher ways of prayer are absolutely impossible if a soul refuses to lose sight of itself and its own efforts. In somewhat the same way, continual contemplation of one's own failings and fruitless endeavours can only lead to discouragement, unless at the same time we keep God and His loving mercy before our mind. The remedy for all such ills is familiar intercourse with Jesus.

It might seem that in thus putting the soul in contact with Jesus, and setting it in conversation with Him on the subject of the meditation, we are merely returning to the "composition of place" and "application of the senses" prescribed in the method. Indeed, there is no reason why we should not do so, to some extent at least, for if we do not steady the sense faculties in some such way, they may upset the whole prayer by their wanderings. But there is a difference of perspective here which would seem to be of importance. Apart from the fact that this way of approach is more spontaneous, and automatically adapts itself to the degree of prayer which the individual soul has reached, it has this particular feature: it puts one in contact with Our Lord as a living Master, Model, and Lover, here and now present to the soul. The importance of this point seems to be capital, and it should make a great difference to the prayer and fervour of many souls.

CHAPTER SEVEN

AFFECTIVE
PRAYER

requent mention has already been made of "affective" prayer, and, indeed, its nature has already been indicated, if only in passing. The subject, however, needs some further treatment. Those familiar with the methodical plan for mental prayer will remember that the consideration of each point was to be followed by certain "acts," and the whole prayer was to terminate in a "colloquy" or conversation with God or with some of His saints. When these acts and the colloquy are extended to take up the greater part of the time of prayer, the prayer is called "affective prayer." It is, therefore, a natural development of meditation, and, in fact, if meditation does not include some affective prayer, it is not prayer at all. There is, therefore, in practice no hard and fast division between the two forms. In affective prayer, the considerations, either on account of long familiarity with the subject or of proper spiritual reading done reflectively, take a small and very secondary place, if indeed they are made at all. A single glance, a moment's reflection, is sufficient to recall and extract all that the subject of the prayer means for us, and the heart commences immediately to express itself in acts, petitions, praise, or any other movements of prayer. To all these actions the name "affections" is given. To understand the term rightly, we must forget completely the association of the English word "affection-ate," for, as we have already noticed, the name is here applied to all those movements of the will towards God which generally manifest themselves in acts of the various virtues. That is the reason why the term "affective" is given to a prayer in which these acts predominate. *It does not, however, indicate any intensity of feeling or emotion.*

Since this type of prayer is a personal audience or a loving conversation with God, it is capable of as many variations as there are persons. Therefore, no hard and fast rules can be laid down for it. The great thing is to talk to Our Lord in one's own words, quite simply, about any topic that is of mutual interest. There should be no attempt at fine words or fine phrases. Not only does Our Lord not look for fine speeches, but He does not even ask for good grammar. In fact, affective prayer is often quite incoherent, one word being used to express quite a multitude of sentiments. For some souls, whose minds are filled with the truths therein contained, the Holy Name of Jesus is sufficient prayer. That one wonderful word says far more than we can ever realise. Other souls cannot find any words to give expression to their desires. They pray somewhat in this manner: "I want . . . I don't know what I want. . . . I just want." And Our Lord understands. He knows that it is Himself that they want, whether they realise it or not. With due allowance for the fact that different temperaments will pray in quite different ways, it may be said that for many, affective prayer will consist in making love to Our Lord. The language of human love, shorn of its grossness, is the only mode of expression that will satisfy the need of utterance that some souls feel. Not every one will pray in this way, but for those to whom it is natural, the finer forms of expression of human love are excellent models for our conversation with Our Lord. He wants to possess our heart, and He wants to give us His Heart, and any words that can help to that end make a perfect prayer. In another way, also, this example of human love may help us to realise how far this prayer can extend. How often is the talk of lovers merely of commonplace things—the tiny little trifles of everyday life—and yet how wrapped up in one another they can be! So, too, in prayer our words and even our subject may be quite commonplace, and yet the love we give and show to Our Lord may be very great.

Other souls, of different temperament, will make use of phrases from familiar prayers, verses of the Psalms, petitions from the Missal, and so on. If the style of the Church's public prayer comes naturally to one, well and good; if not, then no attempt should be made to cast one's prayers in such a style. "Vouchsafe," and other words of that sort, are best left unused. Another way that may help the tongue-tied is that suggested by St. Ignatius of slowly repeating some vocal prayer: the Our Father, the Hail Mary, Soul of Christ, the Litany of the Blessed Virgin, etc. For those who use the Breviary, a single Psalm may be used in this way, with great fruit. One may improvise on it and develop some of the petitions, or may just "free-wheel," so to speak, between the phrases, and let the heart show itself to God without words. Other ways of getting into touch with Our Lord have been indicated in previous chapters, and one's own devotion will find the best way for itself.

There are some errors to be avoided. A common one is endeavouring to do all the talking oneself. The soul should stop now and then and listen to Our Lord. He replies to us, in our conscience, in our heart, often quite unmistakably. Of course, in this matter one should be on guard against self-deception by vain imaginings and "wishful thinking," as the modern phrase has it. A closely-related error is to think that one must keep up a continual flow of words when not listening to Our Lord. As has just been said, we should "free-wheel" in between the acts. The ability to do this is often a good test of our sincerity. Thus, when we have just told Jesus that we love Him with our whole heart, it is only if we are sincere that we can remain silently in that sentiment. Otherwise, we feel compelled to go on saying something, lest we should hear Him saying to us: "If you really loved Me you would not do so-and-so!" That is one of the ways in which Our Lord moulds us to His Heart's desire.

A different type of error is that of trying to *feel* our acts. The essential act of love of God is made in the will and, therefore, unless it overflows into the emotions, it in itself cannot *be felt*. The well-known doctrine of true contrition should be kept in mind in this connection. True sorrow for sin is a turning away of the will from sin, and manifests itself in a determination of the will to avoid it in future. It is quite compatible with a strong animal liking for the sinful pleasure, felt in the lower appetite, and with the consequent pain in giving it up. So, too, in prayer, if our acts proceed from the will, it does not matter whether they affect our feeling or not. As long as we *will* to love God, by that very fact, with the help of grace, we *do* love Him.

Apart from those times when the heart is dry and can produce neither a good thought nor a good word, the chief difficulties in prayer have their roots outside it. This connection which exists between all prayer and the general state of the spiritual life has not yet been dealt with. One point may be mentioned here in connection with affective prayer, for this sort of prayer is especially sensitive to disorders in one's spiritual life. Through a wrong notion of Our Lord and of the correct attitude before Him, some souls have great difficulty in "letting themselves go" and talking to Him quite naturally when at prayer. Now, it is true that reverence is essential to all prayer. But in private prayer we are in converse with a God who is in love with us, and who seeks so great an intimacy with us, and that with such ardour, that He gives us His own Body and Blood for our food, thus showing the intensity of His desire for our heart. He wants us to talk to Him quite freely, and He will make allowances for us if our attention to Him causes us to be unceremonious. Besides, He Himself is the cure for all our ills, and if there is anything wrong with our prayer, such as lack of proper reverence, He can soon put that right. It is better, even at the risk of being wanting in reverence or of being imperfectly disposed, to get into close touch with Him who came to heal our ills than to keep away from Him through an excess of reverence. The last traces of Jansenism are far from extinguished in our notions of piety!

CHAPTER EIGHT

FURTHER DEVELOPMENTS

F rom this point in the ascent of the mountain of prayer there are two ways in which further progress can be made. One is by the simplification of the actual prayer itself at the time set for that exercise. The other is by extending the prayer, so as to weave it into the warp of the whole day's work. These two ways are so closely related to one another that it is best to treat them together. Once prayer has become affective—that is, mainly composed of acts as distinct from reflections—it can and should be often renewed throughout the day by frequent aspirations, which should always be short, often original, and generally in our own words. They may even be quite wordless; a smile, a look, a sigh, a movement of the heart that we ourselves do not even perceive, can speak volumes to such an intimate Friend as Jesus. If this habit be developed, prayer may be maintained throughout our most absorbing occupations, especially if our prayer arises out of the work in hand, in a request for help, for patience in our difficulties, in a word of praise for some particular disposition of God's providence, or if, like St. Philip Neri, one thanks God that things are not going "my way"! The practice of greeting all manifestations of God's will—especially when they are painful—with a smile, even though it be only an interior one, is a prayer of great value, and one that touches the Heart of God in a very special way.

One need not be afraid to spend part of the time of prayer, especially of what may be called voluntary prayer as distinct from those times of prayer marked out for us, saying no word; provided, of course, that no prayer of obligation is thus neglected. For example, a visit to the Blessed Sacrament can be made with few or no words, and if we find a facility in doing so, no consideration of indulgences or other such profit should be allowed to interfere and to lead us to plunge into a long series of repeated vocal prayers, which will only weary the soul, give it a distaste for prayer, and keep it away from Our Lord. Many souls take after Martha, and are solicitous about much speaking and many indulgences when they come to kneel at Our Lord's feet. Mary's is the better part and no consideration of this sort should be allowed to take it away from us. Indeed, if we recall the dispositions necessary to gain the full value of a plenary indulgence, we may realise that the person who spends most of his time quietly at Our Lord's feet is far more likely to gain one at the first attempt than other more "solicitous" souls are to do so by many attempts.

The soul, then, may find itself able to spend some time in a loving thought or regard of God. Prayer of which this is characteristic may be called "simplified" prayer. The term "prayer of simplicity" is often used for such prayer, but, as already mentioned, it is preferable here to avoid the use of this expression. This simplified prayer is a true prayer of very great value, and when fully developed should not be interfered with, either to reflect or to make distinct acts. In practice, while it is a safe rule not to neglect those acts for which one has a facility or an attraction, still, apart from the case of obvious sloth, one should not try to force acts for which there is no facility, but even, perhaps, much distaste—especially when such a disposition is habitual. This is even true of the more arid sort of prayer, where one is holding on to God, to all appearances, by the very finger-tips of the will alone. Acts—short acts—may be necessary from time to time to recover from distractions, but beyond that they should not be forced. In the more consoling phases of this prayer the soul is enjoying God, and this is an exercise of the will very pleasing to Him and most profitable to the soul. If, however, the prayer becomes dry and distracted, and devout affections of any sort well-nigh impossible, then the soul is driven to praying with its will alone. This it does, as Fr. Piny, O.P., writes, "by *willing* to spend all the time of prayer in loving God, and in loving Him more than itself; in *willing* to pray to God for the grace of charity; in *willing* to remain abandoned to the Divine Will. One must clearly understand that if we *will* to love God (leaving aside for a moment the consideration of the part that grace plays in this action), by that very action we actually *do* love Him; if, by a real act of the will, we *choose* to unite ourselves in loving submission to the will of Him whom we love, or desire to love—by that very act of the will, we immediately effect this union. Love is in truth nothing else but an act of the will."

The idea that we can pray without a series of carefully-worded acts is so new to some people that it may be well to discuss it a little further. Authors have recourse to the example of a mother with her child to illustrate this truth. How many unspoken acts of love and admiration does she not make, often quite unknown to herself, as she sits beside the child's cradle! How much does her silence say to the child as she presses it in her arms! Even in human friendship, and still more in human love, the eloquence of silence, the rich expressiveness of a look or of a smile, need no telling. So, too, in our relations with God we can sometimes say all that He wants us to say in silence and repose. This, of course, is not a prayer for all souls, nor for all times. Yet, if we pause occasionally between our acts and just kneel before God in a state of sincere resignation to His will, it will often happen that we find it possible and profitable to remain in this disposition for a short while. If this be the case, let us be assured that then we are really praying, for we are making acts of faith, of hope, and of charity; we are pleasing God, and silently begging His grace and mercy. Prayer made in this fashion may be often possible during visits to the Blessed Sacrament. Those who find a facility in it, and wish for further teaching on the subject, would do well to consult the second part of Fr. de Caussade's work, *On Prayer*, or his smaller book, *Progress in Prayer*.

One advantage of this simplification of prayer is that it becomes easier to extend it into one's working hours. This is a tremendous advance towards the solution of perhaps the most important problem in our sanctification: the sanctification of our day's work. If we sanctify our work we have sanctified ourselves. Of course, there are various degrees of this type of prayer. Sometimes there is no great difficulty in keeping all the faculties occupied with God; they even experience those sensible consolations that God sometimes sends, even to beginners. At other times, the imagination is quite empty and goes off wandering on its own; even the intellect can find nothing on which to fasten. It is only through faith that the will holds on to God. Still, in all these cases it is possible to preserve the essential features of this prayer during one's daily work. The will is turned to God, and the other faculties give expression to that union by doing one's duty, which is, of course, doing the will of God. In this way, our work becomes a real prayer. It is especially when there is question of mental work that the advantages of this form of prayer become most evident.

It is quite possible that the real prayer of many souls who have led a long life of fervour and persevered courageously in their daily meditation is something of this sort. The will is lifted up to God by faith, and, uniting itself to Him by charity, prays to Him in this silent way; the other faculties are carrying out the will of God, either by meditating, or by vocal prayer, or in any other exercise, teaching or manual labour, that His will prescribes. In fact, it would seem that for certain souls, some such occupation for the lower faculties—the recitation of the Rosary or the use of ejaculations, for example—is a necessary condition for the exercise of this prayer of faith. That is why it may often be true that a soul is raised to this degree of prayer, who seems still to be busy with vocal prayer and meditation. There is no need to lay further stress on the advantages of such a prayer of faith, especially for priests or for active religious; they have even more need of it than the members of contemplative orders. With it, they can make their life one continual prayer, so that they can truly say: to work is to pray.

CHAPTER NINE

GOODNESS
OF LIFE

I n previous chapters we have been regarding prayer as the inter-course of a loving friendship with God, and have seen how it can develop and progress in the same way as does the intimacy between human friends. It is true, of course, that prayer is a supernatural act, and is, therefore, completely dependent on the grace of God. This is a part of our subject which we have not yet discussed. But, up to this stage at any rate, the workings of grace are so closely parallel to those of nature, that this view of a "natural" development in inti-macy with God is quite justified.

In passing, we may take occasion of this parallel to notice an error, one more widespread than might be expected, which often sti-fles the growth of prayer. This is the belief that there is no simplified type of prayer after the discursive plodding of a prelude-and-point meditation except those extraordinary occurrences, such as visions and ecstasies, that sometimes accompany the higher stages of con-templation, but which, in fact, are purely accidental and quite unnecessary for the full development of prayer. This is a capital error. Prayer develops just as human intimacy develops, and, like it, has its seasons and its variations. If, therefore, our way of praying is not adapted to the particular state of our intimacy with God, there is bound to be difficulty. If, for example, one is ready and fitted for affective prayer, meditation—that is, discursive prayer—becomes a profitless burden; if, perhaps, one act or one type of act is sufficient to keep the soul occupied at prayer, then any striving to multiply these acts will be found most difficult and disturbing. If the heart wants to speak to God without words, any attempt to force it to make a series of distinct acts may destroy the prayer. Again, if God gives His grace to the will alone, and wishes us to unite ourselves to Him in naked faith, any effort to set the mind or the imagination to work will only be a distraction, and is really a resistance to grace. Then, too, souls who have once reached a high degree of prayer and then fallen into some serious infidelity, cannot resume their former manner of praying without repairing the fault; and though they will not have to climb up the whole of the ladder again, yet their restoration has its own problems. Thus, each degree of intimacy with Our Lord has its proper manner of prayer, and difficulties can arise from failure to choose the right one.

But the greatest difficulties in prayer, and the greatest obstacles to its progress, have their roots outside prayer in the general condition of our spiritual life. On the sincerity of our purpose, the truth of our loyalty, the genuineness of our love—on such things does our prayer greatly depend. Everything that can make or mar friendship and its intimacy will make or mar prayer. We have already noted how the familiarity with God and His teaching that comes from spiritual reading is essential to prayer, and can be a great help for its progress; this, however, is by no means sufficient. The fundamental dispositions from which prayer flows, and on which its progress depends, are: humility, confidence, and a thirst and need for God which shows itself in seeking Him in prayer—and, in fact, at all times by doing His Divine will. Any defect in these dispositions will be reflected in a corresponding failure in prayer.

Prayer will not develop unless the soul is advancing towards the fourfold purity of conscience, of heart, of mind, and of action. As to the first of these, prayer is a loving intimacy with God. Now, this is impossible if the conscience is stained with a deliberate habit of sin, for that is a direct denial of love to God and a definite withdrawal of part of our heart and our life from Him. Even an habitual infringement of a rule, in which we deliberately persist after we have adverted to it, makes it impossible for us to try to look God in the face, so to speak; to go into His presence with that readiness of heart for His service, which is the secret of all true devotion and prayer. That is why it is so important that every priest or religious, and every soul who wishes to advance, should try to look God in the face, in all reverence, at least once every day, without rushing into some form of vocal prayer.

In its perfection, purity of conscience consists in a firm disposition of the will never to consent deliberately to any offence against God or to any departure from His holy will, and is such that, as soon as any act is seen to be opposed to the will of God, it is immediately retracted. Faults of frailty and thoughtlessness will always occur, but we must try more and more to prevent all deliberate faults; and as often as they occur, even be it seventy times seven times in the day, we must so often immediately renounce them and seek God's pardon by a glance of contrition and confidence in His mercy. In this way, we shall gain more in humility than we have lost by our fault, and the confident return to God can give Him more honour than the offence has denied to Him. It is, therefore, an illusion to hope to become a man of prayer while one comes to terms with the enemy. Human weakness and bad habits will cause many a defeat, but the war must be kept up with unceasing courage, and with a grim determination to keep the conscience clean of all that can offend God.

Purity of heart consists in keeping all the affections of the heart for God alone. It is not enough to rule out all sinful attachments, for if our heart is divided by any inordinate attachment, even to lawful recreations, to our work, to persons, or to anything else, we cannot say we love God with our whole heart. There always will be attachments in the human heart, but they must be subordinate to God and to His will, so that they can never usurp His place as the mainspring of our actions. The spiritual life is a love affair with Jesus. He has given us His whole Heart, pouring out for us the last drop of His Blood in the agonising death of the Cross; He demands the whole of our heart, and we cannot refuse to want, at least, to give it all to Him. Without this willingness it is impossible to remain in loving silence before Our Lord. Nothing so darkens our gaze on God, nothing so weakens our desire for God, nothing so lessens our striving for God, nothing so deafens our hearing for God, as a single inordinate attachment. That is the great source of many difficulties in prayer.

Nor are the baneful effects of such attachments confined to this simplified prayer of silence. The very first "act" we try to make at prayer rings hollow and false in our own ears, as soon as we are conscious that we are dividing our heart between God and His creatures. And we cannot be intimate with God for long before He points out to us some of those attachments that cause rapine in the holocaust; for God is a jealous God—He is a consuming fire.

Under purity of mind we include the careful and constant control of our thoughts and memories, by prudently excluding all that is unnecessary, frivolous, and vain; and by gradually building up a continual recollection of God and His works. This is also one of the most important of all mortifications for those who would progress in the spiritual life, and far more effective than the most penitential macerations of the flesh. In fact, without it, corporal penance is almost useless. This internal mortification should be extended to the control of our emotions, especially those of anger, fear, hope, sorrow, and joy. The man whose hope, love, and trust are fixed in God does not give way to anger when God sends him trials or when people try his patience to its limits; nor does he vainly fear God's loving Providence, which he knows covers every single detail of his life. Nor, again, does sorrow at his material losses enter deeply into his heart when it is set on the riches of God; and the joys of this life seem trivial, aye, unworthy even, to one who knows the delight of God's love.

Purity of action, which is often called "purity of intention," consists in a continual watch over the motives which animate our actions, and in a constant effort to act only for the love of God and according to His will. It demands a relentless war on that self-love that is always seeking to inspire all our deeds. When a religious has settled down in the religious life, and has become faithful in his observance of the rule, further progress is to be sought for, not in violent efforts *to* do extraordinary actions, but in an ever-increasing purity of intention in the ordinary works of everyday life. This is the surest way, in fact—apart from very special cases—it is the only way, to fulfil that law of Christian perfection, which St. John the Baptist so well laid down: "He must increase—I must decrease." All search for our own honour, for our own undue ease, all self-seeking, however much it be cloaked by the plea of altruistic motives, or the search of higher sanctity, is directly opposed to that great rule given us by Christ of denying ourselves and following Him.

This, perhaps, may seem too hard, and might lead only to discouragement. But perfection of this fourfold purity is not required for progress in prayer, for such perfection is synonymous with sanctity; we must, however, continually strive towards these dispositions of purity. We must desire this purity, we must pray for it, we must make earnest efforts to acquire it. But without a special help from God, it is unlikely that we should achieve a sufficient measure of it. There is, however, no limit to God's goodness, and it is at this stage that He is accustomed to intervene, taking compassion on our infirmities; after we have been toiling all night and caught little or nothing, He acts through His special Providence, and in a short time He has advanced us beyond all expectation. But He demands that we do our part, that we keep on putting out to sea, so to speak, and persevere in our attempts to make ourselves pleasing to Him and to pray to Him, no matter how fruitless they appear. The perfect picture that St. Teresa of Lisieux has drawn of the spiritual life will help to give us courage. She sees it as a stairway to be climbed, at the top of which God is waiting, looking down in Fatherly love at His child's efforts to surmount the first step. The child, who represents ourselves, fails to manage to climb even the first step; it can only keep on lifting up its tiny little foot. Sooner or later God takes pity on it, and comes down and sweeps the child right up to the top in His arms; but—and St. Teresa insists on this as much as she insists on God's loving kindness—we must keep on lifting up our foot. The soul must never be discouraged by the fruitlessness of its repeated efforts. It seems to be a law of the spiritual life that, since all progress ultimately depends on God, He lets us first learn our complete helplessness by long and weary efforts that come to naught. But we have His word: "I Myself will come and save you!"

CHAPTER TEN

PRAYER AND THE SPIRITUAL LIFE

The discussion of prayer has already been carried far enough to let it be seen that the essential core of prayer is the act of the will, turning to God, seeking God, and uniting oneself to God—to God, be it understood, as known by faith. It is evident, then, that there is a close connection between prayer and the rest of the spiritual life, and that, in fact, as progress is made, the distinction between them tends to disappear, and prayer overflows from the times set apart for it, and begins to penetrate the rest of the day, so that, whether in word or in work, the soul is always lifted up to God in a union of love. This close connection between the different parts of the spiritual life, as well as their mutual dependence, exists from the very beginning. Prayer and practice are really two branches of the same tree of charity. In every tree, the life of each branch depends upon the vital sap that flows into it from the trunk, while the branches in turn supply the whole tree, as well as each other, with food and strength drawn by the leaves from the air and from the sun. So, too, in this tree of charity the branches of prayer and practice depend for their vigour upon the vital sap of grace that comes to them from the supernatural life of the soul; while that life in turn is itself nourished and strengthened by the activity of each branch, for the branches of prayer and practice draw into the whole spiritual organism the riches of the Divine atmosphere and the energy of the Divine sun towards which they stretch forth the leaves

of deeds and desires. In fact, in this tree of charity there is no difference between the roots and the branches; for love grows by loving, and loves by growing.

The way, therefore, which leads to progress in prayer is exactly
the same as that which leads to progress in virtue. That is why
progress in prayer is here being put before priests and religious,
especially before "active" religious, as an integral part of the essential programme of their state. The primary purpose of every religious congregation is not that particular work, such as preaching or
teaching or nursing, which is peculiar to each. It is the sanctification
of each individual member. There is, then, an obligation on each
individual religious to tend to perfection, and this obligation is the
primary duty of his state of life, one which comes before all others.
Therefore, every religious who is really living up to his obligations is
doing all that is necessary to facilitate progress in prayer. More than
that, since prayer is the most powerful means to advance in perfection, and since its power increases with its development, no religious
can dare neglect to try to advance in prayer, nor say that such things
are not for him. Progress in prayer is the result of progress in virtue,
and progress in virtue inevitably follows from progress in prayer.
The more we make our life conformable to the Will of God, the
more facility we find in the practice of prayer. In fact, *the* great difficulty in prayer is that our wills—in other words, our hearts—are
not wholly given to God.

It follows, then, that there need be no hesitation in setting before
priests and before the members of any religious congregation a programme of prayer that leads to, and includes, the higher states of
prayer, even those states that some authors consider to be essentially different from "ordinary" prayer. As far as the effort outside the
time of prayer is concerned, any priest who is living up to the
demands of his office, or any religious who is doing all he is required
to do by his state, is also doing all that is required to make progress
in prayer. If such progress be not noticeable where there is generous fidelity to all duties, it must be remembered that there are many
holy and humble souls who have great gifts of prayer quite
unknown to themselves. Prayer, as we have seen, can become so
"simplified" as to escape the grasp of one's own consciousness.
Further, the ratio between progress and prayer is not the same for
all. Some go far in perfection and, at least, seem to be still in the

elementary stages of prayer; while, on the other hand, God may give some of His best graces to souls who are still far from perfection. Prayer is a means to perfection; it is not perfection itself. One thing may be confidently stated: if more souls set themselves to pray, and to keep on trying to pray better, a far greater number of them would come to their due perfection, and that with less difficulty, than if they treated prayer as some mere incidental exercise of their spiritual life—one which, after all, could be done without. In this matter, members of the more active congregations have no right to consider that prayer such as we now are describing is not for them. It is true, perhaps, that in the contemplative orders it should be easier for souls to advance in prayer; it is true, also, regrettably true, that the day's time-table of some religious is so crammed with work, and that the demands on their energies are so extensive, that little time or energy can be found to develop the interior life. Yet it is nevertheless true that the graces of prayer are offered to active religious just as to everybody else, and that the co-operation needed on their part is nothing more than that to which they are already bound by the essential duty of their state. The legitimate "activities" of religious are no barrier to the work of God's grace; in fact, they are an instrument of that grace, and it may be said that if a religious, after many years in religion, has not reached his due state of perfection in prayer, it is, up to a point, not so much because he is a member of an *active* religious congregation, but rather because his activities have not been as supernaturalized and as interior as is required by his chief duty as a religious.

To facilitate prayer, therefore, and to advance in it, there must be great fidelity to God's will. Rules and all other manifestations of God's desires must be faithfully followed, and the details of the common life as well as one's own daily duties have to be carried out with great exactness and watchful purity of intention. Then, there is need of readiness in corresponding with grace, and of generosity in refusing God nothing for which He clearly is asking. The more one abandons oneself to God's will by cheerfully accepting all its dispositions and lovingly trusting to all its plans, the quicker shall he advance, and the sooner shall the purgative operations of God's action on the soul come to an end. The aim of the soul ought always to be to second God's work for its sanctification. Above all, since humility is the foundation of the whole spiritual life, and since

God wants the soul to be humble at all costs, it should cheerfully and generously accept all the humiliations that He sends to it. This will have another effect, for it removes what is a frequent source of distractions at prayer: the unconscious tendency to try to heal the wounds of our self-love by gratifying thoughts and imaginings, by those foolish dreams and reveries that interfere so much with prayer.

The importance of interior mortification must never be forgotten. There can be no progress in prayer without a mortified life. Now, this does not mean a life of great corporal penance. It is our self-love that we must mortify, and to attempt extraordinary or unusual corporal penances, without a clear call from God, and the approval of some proper authority, is usually only a subtle form of self-seeking. There should, of course, be sufficient corporal penance to keep the body in subjection. The rules and the customs of one's order are the best guide in this matter. Owing to the prominence given by some writers to the extraordinary mortifications practised by some of the saints, many people have got the notion that these things are essential to holiness. The life of St. Teresa of Lisieux is sufficient to correct this error. It must always be remembered that it is by interior mortification of the memory, of the imagination, and of the emotions, and by the ready acceptance of humiliations, that the greatest and the quickest progress is made. To give free rein to one's thoughts, to indulge in reveries, to build castles in the air, to dwell continually on old memories, to nurse one's grievances, to allow wounded pride to dictate one's thoughts or feelings—all such habits are fatal to a life of prayer. No matter what corporal penances be practised, the priest or religious who cannot refrain from airing his grievances and proclaiming his wrongs, looking for sympathy when slighted, and even seeking an opportunity of retaliation, is far from being truly mortified, and, unless he amends, cannot be an intimate friend of Our Lord.

Of great importance is fidelity to the inspirations of grace—to those invitations of the Spirit of God asking for our co-operation in some particular work or sacrifice. It is by these motions of grace that God adapts His plan to, and makes provisions for, the individual needs and circumstances of each soul. They are of especial importance in the spiritual life of a priest in the world. To refuse these invitations, especially to do so habitually, is really to extinguish the Spirit. The whole spiritual life is a partnership with Christ and

His Spirit; prayer is, as it were, the meeting or interview—one might well call it a lover's tryst—where we assure God of our love and of our co-operation, where we manifest our union with Him and even find joy in that union. Now, if the rest of our day gives the lie to our protestations and contradicts our promises, we cannot meet God with sincere sentiments of love or co-operation; thus, prayer becomes "difficult" and even impossible. That, probably, is why so many souls fail to advance far in the way of prayer. It is not because God has refused them the graces of prayer, but because they have refused God that co-operation with what we might call the prayers of His grace—the invitations to work in union with Him—because they have refused Him that co-operation which is the necessary fulfilment and foundation of the sincerity of affective prayer. When we speak to God: we must mean what we say; we must practice what we have promised; we must show forth in work what we say in word.

CHAPTER ELEVEN

THE PATH
OF PROGRESS

There is another consideration which makes it desirable, if indeed it is not also necessary, that the different ways of prayer should be put before every priest and every religious, and this, not merely as speculative knowledge having no relation to practice, but as practical methods of prayer that everyone may have occasion to employ. But it needs some introduction in the form of a discussion of the path by which we ascend to the heights of prayer. It is quite true that there is an age-old division of the spiritual life into three stages—those, namely, of beginners, proficients, and the perfect—dating almost from apostolic times. It is true, also, that progress in prayer has been divided into three ways corresponding to each of these stages. It is further true that the rising path of prayer has been divided into various steps by such great authorities as St. Teresa, and by many theologians of experience and renown. To this tradition of treatment, to this weight of precedent and this example of practice, might be added the kind suggestions of those whose advice was sought in penning these lines, recommending definite division of the spiritual life into well-marked steps with detailed definitions of each type of prayer and classified treatment of the difficulties arising in each class. Yet we have deliberately refrained from too exact an attempt at definition, and also from any clean-cut classification of the different stages in the growth of prayer with well-marked divisions between each stage. In doing so, we do not question for a moment the truth of the principles latent in such a scientific procedure as that of tradition. But this is not a theoretical text-book discussing the difficulties of prayer in general or abstract terms; it is rather an attempt to help individual souls to deal with their own difficulties, and it looks at the spiritual life, not in a scientific, objective manner, but from the subjective point of view of the individual, treating it as it appears to the individual in practice.

Now, if the experience of a large number of souls, of different age, experience, temperament, and time, be taken and averaged out, it will be found that the classical divisions and conclusions are quite accurate and well justified. But, if one were to measure a number of men, take the average of their different dimensions, and make a suit of clothes according to these average measurements, the probability is that there would hardly be any one man whom the suit would fit properly. So it is with prayer. The experiences of each individual, and the way in which it seems to him that his prayer develops, are not to be brought under the letter of a general law. In particular, wide variations will be found in the sequence in which the different degrees of prayer succeed one another. Even in those whose path most closely follows the classical signposts—meditation, affective prayer, simplified prayer, arid contemplation, prayer of union, etc.—these divisions only represent an average over a period in which one particular type of prayer predominated. It is even not impossible that in the stage marked meditation, there were times when each of the other types of prayer were practised. It is unlikely, of course, that all were there. Quite conservatively-minded authors point out that a number of souls start with affective prayer. Many generous beginners have been given, for a short time at least, the graces of contemplation. The task of prescribing for each soul must thus be approached with an open mind, and a full selection of prescriptions.

In addition to this variety apparently inherent in the nature of the case, it would seem that in view of the necessities of these critical times and the fearful strength of the forces in active opposition to Christianity, God is even more ready than usual to pour out His generous graces of prayer on souls who are willing to make use of them. No matter what his state in life, there is hardly any soul who sets himself seriously to the pursuit of prayer and of holiness, of whom it could be said with any confidence that he will not be offered the highest graces of prayer. Therefore, it would seem desirable that every soul should have a practical knowledge of the different ways of praying, and should be prepared to use each according to the varying conditions of grace, of fervour, and of the general weather of his spiritual life. That means that he should be prepared to go up higher if God invites him, and should be ready, with equal cheerfulness and holy indifference to resume the tedious task of meditation, if, all else failing, this should become profitable. That is not to assert that there will be no general development of his prayer; all that has been here written makes it clear that in a healthy spiritual life, some such growth is almost inevitable. But it is very probable that the course of prayer, looked at from day to day, will manifest all sorts of variations and call for a command of various methods. It is noteworthy that St. John of the Cross includes under the one term—that of meditation—the different varieties of prayer that we have been discussing.

That is why exact definitions or clear delineation have been avoided. One can define terms with accuracy; but clear definition of states presupposes the existence of quite distinct and definite divisions in the growth of prayer, which are not so easy to find in practice, especially when looked for in the case of an individual soul. It is even a task of great difficulty to mark out the border-line between the general stage of ordinary prayer and the beginning of what many call infused contemplation. If, therefore, a certain indefiniteness is apparent in the present treatment of the development of prayer, it is because this seems to be more in accordance with the facts of individual experience. That is also why one may feel justified in treating the difficulties of the different ways of praying in an unclassified way.

There is one weapon—one way—that is essential for dealing with all difficulties and for making progress in prayer. That is, a firm resolution never to cease trying, never to give up praying—no matter what difficulties arise, no matter how small the measure of success, no matter what the cost is going to be. When we decide to become men of prayer, we make a declaration of war, not only on our lower selves, but on the devil himself. Nothing but resolute courage and firm unshakeable confidence in God can enable us to persist in that combat. But, if we are generous and do our best, even if that be little more than to glory in our infirmities, then we can be sure of God's assistance, for it is a theological principle that to those who use what little grace they may already possess, God will not refuse His further grace.

There is one difficulty, a most common one, which will test the strength of this resolution; that is, the continual struggle against distractions. These troubles may, of course, have their origin outside prayer, in some attachment, some unmortified curiosity, some morbid brooding over humiliations, for example; they may be due to a failure to recollect oneself generously and completely at the beginning of the prayer. In these cases the remedy is obvious. They may, however, be due to fatigue; for if the powers of the mind are hard at work all day, it is not easy for them to make the effort necessary to remain attentive to what may be a very difficult task. In this case, when the distracting work is of God's appointing and not due to our own self-seeking, we can only glory in our infirmities, and hope in God's grace. Again, distractions may be due to the natural instability of the mind, especially of the imagination. It is a psychological law that one idea tends to call up another, according to the well-known principles of association and contrast, so that the very effort to make one idea clear may be the means of starting a distraction. Distractions, again, may arise from the fact that the subject of our prayer, or the workings of God's grace, make no appeal to the imagination, to our natural tastes, or even to the more familiar part of our intellectual powers. In this latter case especially, the imagination and its attendants seem to run riot, and any attempt to recall them will only draw away the attention from the real prayer, which is going on in the depths of the soul, in what one might call the "invisible light" of faith. In all these cases, all we can do is to renew our attention to God according to the way in which we are praying to Him. This should be done gently and quietly, without vexation, or even without surprise at our own folly.

If we could only realise how much this continual turning back to God shows Him our real love for Him, and pleases Him more than that rapt attention that has its roots in self-love, we should never be dissatisfied with our prayer on account of its numerous distractions. If prayer be a lifting up of the mind to God, then every time we turn away from distractions to renew our attention to God, we pray—and we pray in the teeth of difficulty and despite ourself.

What can be more pleasing to God?—what more meritorious? We should be very greatly surprised if we could get a glimpse at the account book that the recording angel keeps and see the different values he sets on our various attempts at prayer. The prayer that pleased us, and with which we were well satisfied, would often be quite low in his estimate, while the prayer that disgusted us, which was apparently made up of nothing but distractions, might be found to have won a very high degree of his approval.

Sometimes, the mere return to God is sufficient to banish the distraction; but very often the same distracting thought keeps coming back, despite our attempts to get rid of it. One way of dealing with such obstinate intruders is to make them the subject of prayer. With a little ingenuity, some relation can be found between the distracting idea and God. It may, perhaps, give us something to pray for; it may serve as a motive to praise God; it could be used as an evidence of our need for His grace. Whatever it is, God made it, and allowed it to come into our minds, so that there is always some way that leads back from it to God. If all else fails, we can fall back upon the advice of the author of *The Cloud* for dealing with distractions, that we should endeavour to look over their shoulders, as if we were looking at some object beyond them and above them—which is God. There is an excellent chapter on distractions in *Holy Wisdom (Sancta Sophia)*, by Fr. Baker, O.S.B., a work to which these pages owe much, and which is in the same tradition. The part of his book that deals with prayer will be found very helpful, and has been published separately by Dom Weld-Blundell, O.S.B., under the title *Prayer and Holiness*.

Another way of looking at prayer may help us when we feel we cannot pray at all. Let us regard the time of prayer as an appointment with God. If, for His own wise reasons He decides not to keep the appointment, that is His will and, therefore, to be praised. For our part, by kneeling there, helpless, and almost hopeless, we are doing what He wants us to do, and we can confidently leave the result to Him. These helpless half-hours spent fighting sleep and distraction, "getting nowhere," as the phrase has it, have a providential part to play in our sanctification. Distractions which are not deliberate are a trial, not a fault; let us accept them cheerfully and confidently. In His own good time, God will come and save us.

CHAPTER TWELVE

THE DIFFICULTIES
OF NOT PRAYING

So far, we have been considering the difficulties of prayer; we
have also seen that prayer is capable of development, and we
have realised how closely connected it is with the spiritual life, so
that no progress in one is possible without earnest efforts in the
other. Forgetting, perhaps, that he is already bound to these efforts
by the very habit he wears, a religious may allow their apparent difficulty to deter him from seeking proficiency in prayer. Before going
on to treat of any further advance in prayer with its difficulties, it
would be well to see what alternative lies before such a religious.

Quite apart from the fact that the pain and effort involved in the
attempt to advance in the spiritual life bring with them their own
consolation and strength in a more intimate and more conscious
union with Jesus which can rob them of all their hardship, they are
also counterbalanced by the removal of the greatest of all forms of
unhappiness—half-hearted service in religion. To a religious whose
heart is not in his search for union with God, life is a perpetual misery. The whole of the religious life is designed to lead us—to carry
us, in fact—towards that goal of Divine union. Any other course, or
any lagging behind, is continually causing us to rub against the grain
of the whole life, and to pull against its steady stream. If a religious
who thus turns away from the main purpose of his state seeks distraction by getting absorbed in his work, he is continually fretting
against the innumerable obstacles and hindrances that the limitation

57

of his rule of life puts in the way of complete success in that direction. If he tries to find peace in the pursuit of some lower pleasure, he soon finds that he must go to extremes to try to drown the prickings of his conscience and the pangs of that deep-seated hunger of his higher self that can find no food in such folly, and so his days are full of ever-growing misery. Even if he avoids such disorders, the whole round of religious exercises becomes meaningless, senseless, and wearisome in the extreme. He is like a boy at school who does not want to learn, a patient under treatment who does not want to get well, a soldier in arms who is determined not to fight. He is at continual war—if we may dignify his squabbles by that name—with his environment.

The religious state is one in which a soul gives itself to God, and in which God gives Himself to the soul, after He has helped it to sacrifice itself and prepared it for this gift. Any personal plan opposed to this end is completely foreign to the life of that state, and sooner or later, either such a purpose must be given up completely, or else one's failure as a religious has begun. But if one can make one's own the true purpose of that life, and view everything in it as a divinely-planned means of uniting himself to God, then one has found a happiness beyond all telling, and with it the secret of cheerful patience. Many religious, for example, find community recreation a great trial—instead of recreating, it sometimes only irritates. Suppose, however, that one goes to it purely to seek Jesus and to find Him by doing His will, then one has also found a point of view that not only makes the exercise tolerable, but even something that can be accepted cheerfully. In a later chapter we shall see how true it is that by doing God's will, we find God; that even in carrying out what appear to be the most unimportant provisions of the rule, we are doing something which is more pleasing to God and more efficacious for our own eternal happiness than anything else, no matter how great or how heroic, that we could do at that moment. Such an attitude is of very great help in the case of those prescriptions of rule that often seem tedious and unreasonable. Viewed in this way, their fulfilment becomes a constant prayer, a prolonged spiritual communion; not only does it beseech God most effectively to come into our hearts—it actually unites us to Him. Further, it is a fact that by uniting oneself to Jesus in this fashion, by cheerfully doing His will, one is also uniting oneself to all the works of all His servants throughout the whole universe; one is united to each priest saying Mass, to every missioner preaching the Gospel, to every soul praying or suffering for the sake of Christ. Moreover, one partakes of the fruit of their work, and can even share in their reward according to one's loving acceptance of God's will and readiness in carrying out the particular duty God has allotted to him. To seek God truly, to do His will cheerfully, to love Him whole-heartedly—that is the only way to true prayer and to true peace.

Not only is this interior life the only hope of each individual in religion; it is also the only hope of the religious state, and in calling it "the only hope" these words are used in their full meaning. Our Lord, Himself, told His Apostles on the night He ordained them priests and founded the active life of the Church: "Abide in Me, and I in you . . . I am the Vine, you are the branches: he that abideth in Me, and I in him, the same beareth much fruit, for without Me you can do nothing." The whole discourse which He made to them on the night before He suffered was an exhortation to the interior life, and a clear indication that it was the only source of their fruitfulness. In these critical times when the Church has such need of the full co-operation of every one of her religious, it is the interior life of prayer and penance that she needs most, and it sometimes seems as if that is the last help her members think of offering her. There is a danger that under the stress of necessity and through the contagion from a materialistic world, our perspective may become distorted and our scale of values upset. The wonderful works that the religious state has done for the Church and for her members in preaching, teaching, nursing—in all sorts of activity—are one of the glories of Christianity. But all that is but sounding brass and tinkling cymbals if it comes not from a life of prayer and union with God. The temptation to forget this is a strong one. When there is need of new school staffs, when the missions call loudly for help, when the sufferings of the poor tear at our hearts, it is very easy to forget the absolute necessity of a strong, sound, solid foundation in the interior life for every single priest and for every single religious; it is very easy to forget the absolute necessity of sufficient leisure for prayer and for spiritual reading and for the things of the spiritual life. The needs of the moment may crowd these exercises into an ever-shrinking corner of the time-table, make ever-growing claims on the strength and energy of priests and religious, and eventually, may come to fill the whole field of their interest. That would be fatal; for then there can be no more fruit, there can be no more life, since Jesus has been crowded out of the religious life and out of the heart of each religious—He who is the Way, the Truth, and the Life.

To try to gain efficiency, either for the individual or for the institute, by reducing the time or the interest for prayer and spiritual exercises, is even more foolish than to try to get more manual work done by leaving out dinner. All the learning, all the eloquence, all the labour in the world, cannot convert a single soul, unless some one's prayers and sufferings are drawing down the necessary grace. A man's words have no unction unless he is living a life of friendship with Jesus. Boys, for example, will respect a man of high principle, they will learn from a fine teacher, they will even admire a man of penance; but unless he be a close companion of Jesus, no teacher will ever produce that influence on the heart and soul of the pupil that will make him too a friend and lover of Jesus; one might even say that unless someone else is at prayer on his behalf, he will not even make him a good Catholic.

These are but examples of a truth of universal application. The exterior life is worthless unless it flows from an interior life, and no interior life can last long without constant and wholehearted prayer. Now, there is no exercise of the spiritual life that lends itself less to regimentation than prayer, nor is there any which regimentation so quickly blights and withers. Prayer should be the most spontaneous practice of all. Its healthy development in a religious congregation is best assured, not by over "organisation" with fixed methods and matter, but by first of all forming in each religious the spirit of the interior life with a strong conviction of its value and necessity, by leading him to intimate intercourse with Jesus, and by then giving him ample opportunity and every encouragement to develop it.

CHAPTER THIRTEEN

THE PRAYER
OF THE PRIEST

S o many references have been made in previous chapters to the
religious life that some consideration must now be given to the
case of the priest living in the world. It must not be thought that all
that is said in this book about the possibility of progress in prayer is
one whit less true for the priest than for the religious. The only reason why more detailed reference has here been made to the religious life is because this book is written by a religious, and it is only
questions of which one has immediate experience that one can
effectively treat in detail. It seemed better for a writer who can only
have second-hand knowledge of the priest's problems to avoid treating his difficulties in too much detail lest they should not receive full
appreciation and understanding. These difficulties are such that a
cloistered contemplative who would try to deal with them too
minutely might easily betray himself as an armchair strategist.

Yet some reference must be made to these problems, otherwise it
might seem that prayer and perfection were not considered feasible
for priests in the world. Now, on the contrary, progress in prayer is
not only possible for them—it is even of capital importance for them
precisely because, as priests, their functions call for perfection.

Even though the last chapter drew its conclusions from the fact
that the primary duty and purpose of the religious state is to tend
to perfection, there is no need for us here to discuss the perfection
of the priestly state precisely as a *state*. Whether the text of St.

Thomas that has led to some difference of teaching in this matter applies to present-day conditions is a question that need not be settled here. (Those who wish to examine the point will find it discussed in *The Secular Priesthood* by Dr. E. J. Mahoney.) St. Thomas is quite definite in stating that the functions of the priest, whatever his "state," require greater interior sanctity than even the religious state (cf. St. Thomas, *Summa*, II-II, 184, a. 8). The pronouncements of the recent Popes leave no room for doubt about the necessity of sanctity in the priest. It will suffice here to quote Pius X: "There are some who think and teach that the whole value of a priest consists in the fact that he devotes himself to the needs of others. How false and disastrous is such a doctrine. Personal sanctity alone will make us the kind of men demanded by our Divine vocation: men crucified to the world, men to whom the things of the world are dead, men walking in the newness of life." *(Haerent Animo*, August 4th, 1908.) Succeeding Pontiffs have only reaffirmed this principle.

It is true that a priest is not bound to the use of exactly the same means of perfection as a religious, but that does not lessen his obligations, for the fact is, that while the religious state is a way to perfection and therefore open to those who are still far from holiness, the priesthood actually presupposes that one has already acquired holiness. (Cf. St. Thomas, *Summa*, II-II, 189, a. I, *ad* 3.) One might say, in fact, that whereas a religious is bound to tend to perfection by reason of his state, the priest is only bound to do so if he has not already attained the perfection required by his priesthood; his primary obligation is to *be* perfect.

Reference has already been made to the words used by Our Lord Himself in addressing the Apostles after He had ordained them priests. They are so full of light on the present subject that they may be quoted again in full:

> "Abide in me, and I in you. As the branch cannot bear fruit of itself, unless it abide in the vine, so neither can you, unless you abide in me. I am the vine: you the branches: he that abideth in me, and I in him, the same beareth much fruit: for without me you can do nothing. If anyone abide not in me, he shall be cast forth as a branch, and shall wither, and they shall gather him up, and cast him into the fire, and he burneth. If you abide in me, and my words abide in you, you shall ask whatever you will, and it shall be done unto you. In this is my Father glorified; that you

bring forth very much fruit, and become my disciples." (St. John xv. 4–8)

And almost as if He had looked down the long years and had heard us protesting: "But, Lord, how shall these things be? We must live in the world, we must live with the world; so that many and immense are the difficulties that hold us back from such perfection!"— He gives utterance to the whole truth of the power and success of His mission as our Saviour in a word that is a perfect answer to any difficulty that a priest may find in achieving holiness:

"In the world you shall have distress: but have confidence, I have overcome the world." (ib. xvi. 33)

That is why it can be confidently asserted that everything which has been written in these pages about the possibility and the need of progress in prayer and in perfection for religious applies *a fortiori* to those whom Our Lord has chosen as His friends rather than as servants and has made the salt of the earth, namely, the priests of His Church. For, once it is clear that a priest is bound to perfection, it follows that it must be possible for him to achieve it, no matter what difficulties may lie in the way or what special graces he may need to do so. In this connection, the words which Our Lord used to sum up the spiritual life of His priests are full of significance; for how can one "abide" in Christ if not by a life of prayer?

This point has been stressed at some length because it gives a remedy for the first great difficulty that priests experience in perseverance in prayer, namely, the persuasion that comes to them sooner or later, that progress in prayer is not possible for *them*—that the higher stages of prayer are only for chosen religious. The whole of this book can be taken as an answer to that objection. Priests, in fact, have so much in common with religious in this matter that a summary of some of the difficulties that may occur in the prayer of clerical readers will find a general application.

The first difficulty—due to the notion that success is not possible— has already been dealt with. A second difficulty is that due to the want of proper spiritual reading. Such reading is an essential food for a life of prayer. It must be suited to the needs of the individual, and not done merely for the sake of knowledge, for preaching, or for the purposes of direction. It is because of the lack of such reading that one often has to insist upon daily methodical meditation instead of encouraging souls to pray.

Thirdly: many fail in mental prayer for want of a grim determination—it must be grim, especially in the case of a priest living in the world, if it is to prevail—never to give up the practice of spending, say, at least half an hour daily in an attempt to pray, *no matter how unsuccessful that attempt may seem to be.* Even if the result is nothing but distractions or drowsiness, the resolution to persevere must not be relinquished. There is always the danger that when a priest who has to plan his own day considers the numerous urgent calls upon his time and the many—and apparently more profitable—purposes to which he could devote the period seemingly wasted in a fruitless attempt at prayer, he may yield to the temptation to abandon such a practice. That would be fatal. Every priest should appoint some set time for daily prayer, preferably in the morning before Mass, but if necessary, in the evening, and make it a strict rule never to fail at least to try to pray then for, say, half an hour. If the evening is chosen as more suitable, it would be well to give a short period to informal prayer in the morning, in order to enter into partnership with Our Lord for the work of the day. The mind of the Church about the priest's mental prayer is reflected in Canon 125. One may say that the fruitfulness of the whole day's work depends upon this attempt at prayer, so that it must never be permanently set aside on the plea of making a better use of the time given to it. There is no better use possible.

Still another cause of failure is indicated by the fact that many give up mental prayer, or at least fail to advance in it, because of their belief that mental prayer means methodical meditation and nothing else. When such meditation becomes almost impossible, they either give up all attempt at mental prayer, or else persevere by heroic efforts in the use of the "method," when they should proceed to pray without method. At most, a method is only one way of praying, but generally it is merely a means to *prepare* to pray; it is not always successful or even helpful, and in such a case it should be left aside.

There is also the kindred error of believing that there is no form of prayer between such meditation and passive contemplation. A somewhat similar difficulty can arise from too rigid a notion of the division of progress in prayer into three or more very well-marked stages. One is afraid, say, to make use of simplified prayer because one's virtues seem to be too imperfect. Or, perhaps, one is deterred from using a simplified form of prayer, by the impression received from some authors who speak of a mystic state of prayer which they call the prayer of simplicity, and which, in their opinion, presupposes that the soul has passed through certain classical stages of purification called "dark nights." At other times we meet the opposite error of refusing to return to a lower degree of prayer when that is necessary.

These difficulties find their solution in what has been written in previous pages on progress in prayer. In particular, stress must be laid on the fact that the individual's path of progress is not bound to follow any general law. Prayer should be taken as it comes, without worrying too much about what "degree" it is, or at what "stage" one has arrived. In fact, for the individual at any particular moment, such "locations" are often quite misleading and can even be completely meaningless.

No one can deny the fact that a priest has his own special difficulties, both in his spiritual life and in his mental prayer—difficulties that are generally much greater than those of religious. The religious life is sheltered; it is designed to lead to perfection, and even its smallest details are directed by obedience. The religious knows at each moment what God's will is for him, and the doing of that will is the mainstay of his spiritual life and the foundation of his prayer. The priest on the mission has not that detailed knowledge of God's plan in his regard—but he has God's Holy Spirit, and he must live by Him. Attention and fidelity to the inspirations of the Holy Ghost and to the obedience of charity may replace for him the obedience of the religious state. In fact, one might say that devotion to the Holy Ghost should be one of the main features of the priest's spiritual life. The Holy Ghost was given to him in ordination for all the needs of his priesthood. Personal sanctity and prayer are among those needs. Our Lord has made all fruitfulness depend upon our "abiding" in Him; the Holy Ghost is the principle of such a union.

This partnership with Our Lord is also a feature which should characterize the life of a priest. The priest's union with Our Lord is so close that he consecrates and absolves in the first person: "This is *my* body; *I* absolve thee . . ." A true conviction of his own powerlessness and his constant need of help will soon lead him to a vivid sense of partnership with Jesus. This will be fostered by recollection and by frequent aspirations to his Divine Saviour who is the source of all his strength and confidence. One way of giving expression to this partnership in prayer is by frequent use of verses from the Psalms of the breviary as aspirations in private prayer. Such words are an inspired expression of prayer, and can be uttered in the name of Christ and of His Church. They will often be of help at mental prayer for they can also express our own needs. The Psalms are full of petitions for mercy, cries of confidence in God, and praise for His goodness that should come so fittingly from our lips. Who is there, for example, that cannot apply to himself the words of the *De profandis?*

Much more could be written on the possibilities of building the spiritual life of the priest on a constant partnership with Jesus, but enough has been said to make it clear that there is no reason why clerical readers should not apply to themselves without reserve all that is here written of progress in prayer and in perfection. They have their own difficulties, but have not they a better right than anyone else to make their own the confident words of St. Paul: "Gladly therefore will I glory in my infirmities, that the power of Christ may dwell in me" (II Cor. xii. 9)?

CHAPTER FOURTEEN

THE INDWELLING
SPIRIT OF ADOPTION

Our discussion of prayer has led us into a consideration of other parts of the spiritual life. This is not a vain digression for prayer is the flower which grows on the tree of the whole of a man's life; to ensure its soundness we must look to the whole plant, and to every part of it. That is why we must now go on to consider the spiritual life in general, and to examine it from a point of view that may help us to pray.

The end of all prayer is union with God. It might also be said that union with God is the beginning of all prayer, just as it is the beginning of the spiritual life. The wonderful effects of Baptism, which is the initiation into the life of the spirit, are too often unknown or forgotten. That is a tremendous loss, for it is by this Sacrament that we are made children of God in truth as well as in name. In Baptism it is not a mere extrinsic adoption which has no inner effect on us that takes place, but there is a real intrinsic change produced in our soul by which we are made partakers in the divine nature, especially in the divine sonship, so that we can truly call God Our Father. More than that: in Baptism, God comes to dwell in our hearts really and truly, in a manner quite different from that in which He is present in the rest of creation. He takes up His abode in us in such a way that we can know Him and love Him in an entirely new and wonderful manner.

In Our Lord's own instructions on prayer He insisted on our
addressing God as a Father . . . "pray to your Father . . . the Father
knoweth you have need of these things . . . thus shall you pray—
'Our Father.'" If we but remember that as long as we are in the state
of grace, there is that in us which makes us sons of God, sons in
reality, not merely in name—if we remember also that God is a
Father to whose goodness, to whose "Fatherliness," there is no limit,
our confidence at prayer will have a sure and solid foundation. Our
mere attitude on our knees, or in any posture of prayer before God,
becomes a prayer in itself; our needs, our weakness, our failures, our
infidelities, even our sins, become our most eloquent entreaty to His
Fatherly compassion and can draw down on us His infinite mercy.
God will not turn away from a contrite heart, and a troubled spirit
is not merely a prayer—it is a sacrifice in His eyes. This reliance on
our sonship finds fresh foundation when we realise that our needs
cry out to God, not merely as our own, but as those of Christ; for,
as we shall shortly see, such is the union of Christ with our soul that
in these things He forms, as it were, one person with us in the eyes
of His Father.

There is no need to recount all the texts of Sacred Scripture that
support this confidence; Our Lord's own parable of the Prodigal
Son is more than sufficient, for it shows clearly how far one can
press this claim of sonship. Even if we have wasted all our substance
in riotous living, we can still arise and go to Our Father, admitting
before Him that we have sinned; if Our Lord's parable means anything, it must mean that we can be absolutely certain that the Father
will come to meet us, even when we are afar—it must mean that our
mere coming in and kneeling down before Our Father against
Whom we have sinned, is a prayer that will move Him to the heights
of His infinite mercy and goodness. If a burning candle before a
plaster statue can express the prayer of a trusting soul, how much
more the presence of a contrite sinner at the feet of his heavenly
Father, especially if distraction and dryness rob him of all sight and
feeling of that Father's goodness, so that he can find nothing to rely
on except the unfelt hope of a grim act of faith!

St. Paul throws more light on this wonderful gift of sonship, for
he assures us that it is conjoined with the presence of the Holy Ghost
Himself in our souls. Not only does the Holy Spirit give testimony
that we are the sons of God, but since without Him we cannot as

much as say even the name of Jesus meritoriously, He prays within us and for us with an ineffable prayer—the prayer of God Himself. This profound doctrine of the presence of the Holy Ghost in the souls of those who are in the state of grace, and of His co-operation with their actions, is far from being realised by even educated Catholics. But when we consider all His functions in our soul, we are astounded, for it would seem that He is there as our possession and for our use!

Fruitful as further consideration of this wonder for our spiritual life would be, one cannot here do more than note its connection with prayer. About this, St. Paul is quite explicit. In the Epistle to the Romans, he writes: "Likewise the Spirit also helpeth our infirmity. For we know not what we should pray for as we ought; but the Spirit Himself asketh for us with unspeakable groanings. And He that searcheth the hearts, knoweth what the Spirit desireth; because he asketh for the saints according to God." If, then, the Holy Ghost assists our infirmity, should we not glory in our infirmities so that the prayer of the Spirit may rise unimpeded from the hidden depths of our souls? Why should we despair at the coldness of our hearts and the failure of our words, when we have within us the very Person of God Who is Himself the love of the Father and the Son, by whom we cry "Abba—Father!"? It is clear, then, that it is no mere empty figure of speech to say that our very presence before God—however helpless we feel, however speechless we are—can in itself be a prayer that touches the heart of God, just as a child can touch its parent's heart by its very helplessness and misery without needing to utter a single word.

These considerations should give us confidence in prayer, no matter at what stage of the spiritual life we may be. In passing, it should be noticed that there is no need to look for God outside ourselves when we wish to pray. Every soul in the state of grace has God within him, seeking his friendship, his confidence, and his love. A mere act of attention puts us in touch with Him, a mere thought is sufficient to speak to Him, a mere movement of the heart gives Him our love. But God has not come into our souls merely to be inactive there. He comes to help our infirmity, and when sanctifying grace is poured into our soul by the Sacraments or in any other way, the Holy Ghost comes to us to abide with us, and not only gives us the infused virtues of faith, hope, and charity, with the moral virtues

as well, but also endows us with His Seven Gifts: wisdom, understanding, counsel, fortitude, knowledge, piety, and the fear of the
Lord. We may regard all these riches, which are beyond all valua-
tion, as a new supernatural organism, as it were, by which we are
enabled to live a new life in accordance with our new nature as sons
of God. The whole of the spiritual life consists in the development
and growth of this new life—the "new man," as St. Paul calls it—
and the subjection of all our own nature, the "old man," to the life
of the new. This explains the continual internal combat that St.
Paul refers to so vividly. The difficulty of this new life is clear when
we remember that it is a life of faith, not one of feeling. But that
should in no way cause us to hesitate, even for a moment, before
devoting ourselves with our whole heart to its claims. For, as Our
Lord Himself has promised, we are given another "paraclete," that
is a "comforter," one who strengthens us, and it is God himself with
His omnipotent power who thus comes to be our permanent help,
our aid, and our strength. Therefore, no difficulty, real or imaginary,
should ever make us hesitate to embrace a life of prayer. We are
never conscious of all the strength at our disposal, but as each occasion arises, God's power becomes available for our use if we but act
with faith, with confidence, and with humility.

Above all, the absolute and essential necessity of humility for
progress in prayer should be emphasized. God made the world for
His own glory, and He will not give His glory to another. Now, in
this life, He glorifies Himself by the works of His mercy, by taking
compassion on our infirmity, by raising us up out of the dust to
share in His own nature, in His own strength, and in His own joy.
All the works of our supernatural life come from Him. Even the fact
that they belong to us in such a way that we can merit by them is
due entirely to His gracious mercy. If, therefore, we glory in anything else but our infirmities, we take to ourselves something to
which we have not the slightest claim, something which belongs
entirely to God, for He it is who worketh in us both to will and to
accomplish. Our pride robs God of the credit for His work—work
that in His goodness He performed in such a way as to be available
for our merit—for we have nothing which we have not received, not
even our merits.

God is more interested in our salvation and our progress than
we ourselves are. He is our Father and is always so, actively. That is

to say that He will sanctify us and unite us to Himself, as long as we put no obstacle in His way. Now, the greatest of all obstacles is our pride, for by it we turn His saving action on us against His purpose in creating and ruling the world, which purpose is His own glory. Thus we make ourselves enemies of God, and therefore it is written: "God resisteth the proud and to the humble He giveth His grace." St. Benedict's rule is of great significance in this connection. Writing a rule for a contemplative order, in which men of prayer were to be formed, the holy Patriarch has only a few short words to say of prayer, nor does he treat of the rest of the spiritual life at any greater length until he comes to write of humility. On that subject he is eloquent and insistent, ascribing to it the properties of a ladder by which one can reach the heights of the spiritual life; and St. Thomas Aquinas follows his example, giving first place to humility in the removal of the obstacles to God's action on the soul.

Here one can do little more than merely mention these tremendous truths of the inhabitation of God in our souls. To treat them adequately would need a whole book. To do less would be to run the risk not merely of misrepresentation, but of caricature. The reader himself must seek their development elsewhere. The Epistles of St. Paul are replete with this doctrine; it is fundamental in his teaching. A very fine and readable summary of this subject, and of the closely-related one which is the subject of the next chapter, will be found in the opening part of Tanquerey's *The Spiritual Life*. This work, which has been translated into English, is a mine of information on every part of the spiritual life and should be in the library of every religious house, even of those who have not been trained in theology. It is the outstanding work of reference on the spiritual life. A smaller work by Fr. Plus, S.J., *God Within Us*, will be of great help. The next chapter will indicate other sources of information.

The use of this doctrine of the presence of God within us as a basis of prayer finds support in the teachings of St. Teresa. In one place she tells us that the soul has no need to seek God outside itself to pray to Him. He is within, and may be addressed with all the simplicity of a child speaking to its father. We should tell Him our needs and our troubles, and beg Him to remedy them all. The Saint appears to consider this to be one of the best ways of ensuring rapid progress in prayer.

In another place she insists on the advantages of forming a lively conviction of the close presence of God. She tells us that she herself did all she could to remember and realize continuously the
presence of Our Lord within her. If she was meditating on a mystery, she represented it to herself within, and addressed all her
"affections," or acts, to her Divine Guest. This way of remembering God can be very profitably joined to the manner of praying
known as the second method of St. Ignatius. This is done by reading or reciting some prayer very slowly, pausing after each word or
phrase to grasp its meaning in our mind, to excite its reality in our
heart, to develop it in variations or to insist on it in silent assent,
according to our inclination, and to do all this addressing ourselves
to Our Lord and our Master, our Guest and our Saviour, our Lover
and our God, who is within us. Such a way of praying to God in our
hearts can be employed with great profit at the Rosary or at the
Divine Office.

Nor are words necessary. We may be content with paying silent
attention to our guest, confident that He sees and accepts the love
and worship that is in our heart. The two essential features to be
attended to are the interior reference of our prayer and its unforced
utterance; we should never forget St. Teresa's statement that
"Mental prayer is nothing else but an intimate friendship, a frequent
converse, heart to heart, with Him whom we know to be our Lover."

CHAPTER FIFTEEN

OUR IDENTIFICATION
WITH JESUS

I f a man commit a crime or do someone an injury, his friends can, of course, do a lot to help him. They can repair the injury he has done; they can appease the anger of the person injured; they can help the man himself to do both of these things; they can encourage him and plead for mercy for him. But they cannot, in strict justice, relieve him of liability to punishment by undergoing the punishment themselves, nor can they wipe out the stain of his guilt. Guilt, punishment, and merit are personal things; they cannot be dealt with vicariously. In the strict sense, no man can take another's guilt on himself; no man can merit, or be justly punished, for another. How then did Our Lord save us? How then did He avert the punishment that was due to us? How did He merit for us? How did He come to suffer for our sins? The most satisfactory answer to these and many similar questions is found in the pages of St. John and St. Paul. St. John gives us Our Lord's own words: "I am the Vine, you are the branches." St. Paul insists again and again: "You are the Body of Christ."

To sum up and explain the doctrine so vividly expressed in these two phrases is no easy task. The truth on which it rests is so rich, so wonderful, so deep, so unparalleled, that it must be looked at from many different points of view and a synthesis made of the various— almost contradictory—ideas so obtained, before one comes to a reasonably complete grasp of its nature. Only a few partial presentations of the truth can be given here, but they will suffice for our purpose.

In the Incarnation, God the Son, the Second Person of the Blessed Trinity, united to Himself hypostatically a human nature, so that Jesus Christ, the Son of Mary, was truly God and truly Man, one person with two natures. That, however, was not the end of the process of union with the human race. The words of St. John's Gospel and of St. Paul's Epistles make it clear that Our Saviour wished to enter into a real but mysterious union with each member of the human race, and that He actually does unite each human being to Himself at Baptism so as to form with Him, one thing, one body, one man, one mystical Christ. From certain points of view we could almost regard this union as forming one person, but it must be clearly understood that we do not lose our individuality in this union. Still, the union is so close that Christ can suffer in all justice for our sins, and we can in all justice use His merits as our own. The controversies with heresy which have taken up such a great part of the work of theologians in the last few centuries, have tended to draw attention away from this tremendous doctrine of our incorporation in Christ; so much so that, to some, this statement of it may seem too vigorous. The Fathers, however, especially St. Hilary, St. Cyril, St. John Chrysostom, and St. Augustine, are far more vehement and vigorous in their utterances. St. Thomas Aquinas, whose words were measured with the precision that is the hall-mark of that prince of theologians, simply asserts that in Baptism the sufferings of Christ are communicated to the baptised person—who becomes a member of Christ—in such a way as if he himself had suffered all that pain. And he answers the questions which were put at the beginning of this chapter concerning the way in which Christ satisfies for our sins by stating that He does so through the fact that we are the members of Christ and form with Him one body and even, in this matter, one person; and that, therefore, the satisfaction offered by Christ applies to all the faithful since they are members of Himself. He sums up the doctrine by saying that the actions of Christ belong not only to Himself, but also to all His members, with the very same relation which the actions of a just man have to the individual agent. (Cf. *Summa, III;* q. 48, *art.* 1 *and* 2.)

Another way of stating the doctrine is to say that we are *"in Christ."* St. Paul uses the phrase one hundred and sixty-four times; and it must certainly be taken as more than a mere metaphor. The Fathers try to illustrate the relationship by comparing it to the union of a drop of water with the wine into which it has fallen. They say, too, that we are in Christ and filled with Him, just as a glowing iron or coal put into the fire is in the fire and is part of it. Our Lord's own example of the vine shows our position even more clearly, for just as the vital sap flows from the vine into its branches, so He sends His Spirit into our souls and we are vivified and divinised—the word is not too strong—by grace, which is a participation in His nature.

There is still another way of regarding this wonderful work of divine love. We can truly say, as St. Paul does say, that Jesus Christ is *in* us. He abides in our souls as long as we are in the state of grace, and, as far as we allow Him, shares our every action. This aspect of the doctrine has been very well treated in the little work by Fr. de Jaegher, S.J., to which reference has already been made, and which has appeared in English under the title *One With Jesus*. This little book, hardly more than a pamphlet, will open up for many readers a rich mine of undreamt-of possibilities. It should be familiar to every soul who takes the spiritual life at all seriously. In it, we can see how Jesus lives in our hearts—how we can pray to Him there, and pray with Him there; in it we can read a glowing account of the burning desire in the Heart of Jesus to share our every thought and deed, to give each one of us a share of His own life and merits and love. The book itself must be read, but the mere idea here given of it is sufficient indication of what possibilities it opens up for prayer.

The results of this doctrine of our incorporation—our identification, if we may use the word—with Christ, which we have indicated in merest outline, are wide and far-reaching. Our Lord's injunction to pray in His name takes on a new significance. We can remind the Heavenly Father of His Son's promise that whatsoever would be done to the least of His brethren would be done to Himself, and we can put our own needs before the Father as those of Christ Himself, in all truth and all reality. We can ask for every necessary or helpful grace for ourselves as for Christ Himself, because it is for the purpose of developing His Life in us that we need it. More than that: we know that Jesus Himself asks for us and with us. That is why we can take Our Lord's words quite literally when He says: "Amen, amen, I say to you: if you ask the Father anything in My Name He will give it to you." Behold, then, the ground of the absolute confidence with which we must go to the throne of grace. No sin, no shame, should ever make us hesitate to approach God in prayer.

If Jesus thus takes our part in our prayers and works, we also take part in His. Here we have a principle that can be of great help when we are "paralysed" at prayer. Our union with Jesus is such that, as long as we do not break it by a deliberate sinful motion of our will, we may always lay claim to a share in His merits and in the good works that He is doing in all the other members of the Church, for we are all one Body in Christ. We can even share in His prayer to the Father in heaven. Obviously, the extent of our participation depends on the closeness of our union with our Head. The most perfect union is that of the will, and when we are doing the will of God for the love of God, we are then most closely united to Him. No matter, therefore, how helpless or how hopeless seem our attempts at prayer, if we but do His will, if we put ourselves on our knees at His command, we can count on a great share in His prayer, for He is living at the right hand of God, always making intercession for us.

Prayer is a work of partnership between Jesus and each one of us. Our part in the partnership lies in doing His will and conforming ourselves to it, and the limitations of our efforts are part of that will. If we carry out our part, we can claim the whole fruit of our joint efforts. If, in particular, we go to prayer resigned to God's will and to our own helplessness, we need not be discouraged at our apparent lack of success; Our Lord is our "Supplement" in all these things, and supplies for all that we are not able to do. Moreover, our powerlessness is part of His plan to make us rely on Him.

It thus appears that, as regards prayer, our union with Christ is of more importance than our fluency or our feeling of fervour, and matters more than our freedom from distraction. If distractions, therefore, are involuntary, but are accepted as a trial permitted by God for His own wise ends, then, in so far as they unite us to Christ by suffering in accordance with the will of God, they are a help rather than otherwise to our prayer. Actually, if a soul goes to prayer in order to give itself to God, with its mind made up to attend to God and to nothing else as far as it can do so, and is resigned to whatever trials or aridity or distraction that Providence permits, its prayer, even though it seems to be a complete failure and almost a waste of time, is nevertheless a most pleasing holocaust in God's sight, which will bring down many graces upon the soul and advance it much towards union with God.

It further follows that every action of the day, no matter how "active," if done according to God's will, is done in union with Christ, and is not only a prayer in itself, but is an excellent starting-point either for one of those wordless colloquies or for a more articulate conversation with Jesus which can make our whole day a time of prayer. It is impossible to work in such close companionship with Jesus and not pray to Him. On the other hand, of course, if our actions are not in accordance with His will, His company is rather an embarrassment, and thus self-will kills a life of prayer.

The continuous and intimate presence of Jesus in our hearts means that no place or occupation is an obstacle to prayer. We are not compelled to go outside ourself to find the God to whom we wish to speak. We are not compelled to hide our working clothes, so to speak, nor to cease from our week-day labours, before we put ourselves in His presence. Not only is He already present wherever we may be, but He is actually sharing our work—so that our work is rather a means of prayer than an obstacle to it. This does not mean that there is no need for some period of the day when we can leave everything else aside to recollect all our powers and turn them to Him. It means rather that there is a prayer for all times—that the hearts seeking God can pray to Him now by words, now by works, now by silence, now by speech.

Not only is Christ to be found in ourselves, He may also be found and served and prayed to in our neighbour. Everything we do for our neighbour is done to Jesus. Once we understand that prayer can be most informal, we can easily see how any contact with our fellow-men can be turned into prayer to Jesus. Further, it is significant that before Our Lord made such extraordinary promises about the efficacy of prayer, He laid down the new commandment of mutual charity, and illustrated it by washing the feet of His disciples. Therefore, we may conclude that we cannot pray in union with Him unless we are united to our fellow-men by charity. He even insisted that before offering sacrifice we should go and be reconciled to our brother whom we have offended.

Thus, all that we do in word or in work can be a prayer. The very food we eat is given to Jesus, for what we do to ourselves we do to Him. Even our pleasures can be His delight. We cannot take a walk that He does not share and enjoy; there is no part of our life, whether it be work or play, in which He does not join, as long, of course, as it is according to the will of the Father.

Thus, the soul in the state of grace can in a way imitate the priest at Mass, who at the end of the Canon holds up the Chalice and the Host and prays to the Father through Christ, saying: "Through Him, and with Him, and in Him, is to Thee, God the Father Almighty, in the unity of the Holy Ghost, all honour and glory." In this way, by showing forth Christ in our lives through doing the will of God, we sing the new canticle of honour and glory, which is Christ Himself.

CHAPTER SIXTEEN

THE GROWTH
OF JESUS WITHIN US

In the last chapter were set forth some different aspects of the wonderful mystery of our incorporation in Christ. It is left to the reader to choose that which attracts him and to develop it by reading and reflection, by prayer and by practice. Some further consideration of the subject may be of help. We saw that Jesus comes into our souls at Baptism, there to dwell in a loving and living union with us. It is also true to say that He *grows* in our soul. The extent to which He participates in all our life depends greatly on our will. He does not take away our freedom; we can live our own life if we wish. If we do so to such an extent as to commit mortal sin, we banish Him from our soul. But even those actions which, without being seriously sinful, are yet not in full accord with His will, reject Him from as much of our life as they include. Therefore, we can speak of the growth and of the formation of Christ in us, according as more and more of ourself and of our activities are subjected and handed over to Him. Obviously, one single deliberate *habit* of infidelity spoils the sense of companionship with Jesus, and thus prevents prayer. We cannot take only a part of our lives and give it to Him, and, having forgotten Him, or even put Him aside, for the rest of the day, expect then to face Him without difficulty or embarrassment when we do decide to advert to His presence. Despite His clemency and His patient kindness there will be awkward pauses in the conversation; certain subjects must be avoided; protestations of devotion which hardly harmonise with our neglect and rejection will sound hollow, and will even die away on our lips. At times we will talk wildly and hastily in order to rush over some unfortunate memory, and since we have made up our mind that on certain points we will not give Him what we know He wants, we cannot catch His eye or look in His face with that quiet smile of complete surrender that comes from a heart ready to give Him all that He asks for, and which is perfect prayer. That is the great difficulty in prayer. We want to meet God on our own terms; we want to make a compromise; we want to work with Him at certain times and in certain ways, but, to put it crudely, we want to be rid of Him in other circumstances. That is just the trouble. One cannot get rid of Our Lord for a time. He is there all the time, and one either treats Him as a permanent friend, or else one has a "difficulty" in prayer.

Further, even though we do try to give Him a place in our company at all times, we may try to forget that He is a crucified God; that He never did His own will; that He always denied Himself; that He delivered Himself; that He emptied Himself, becoming obedient unto the death of the cross. We should like to have Him, but we do not want to share *all* His ideals, to follow *all* His ways, and thus again we find prayer "difficult." No wonder! For if prayer be essentially an awareness of God, all that makes us unwilling to be aware of Him is an obstacle to prayer. There lies one of the roots of the connection between mortification and prayer. Unless we are at least willing that He should teach us His ways, even the way of the cross, we cannot meet Him in prayer with that feeling of open, frank, and unreserved loyalty which is so essential to friendship.

It must be clearly understood that it is the habitual and deliberate opposition to the desires of Jesus that is such a serious obstacle to prayer. No matter how often or how far we fall, Jesus is always ready to renew our union, as soon as we are again determined to give up our own way. In fact, as we have seen, there is a type of love and understanding that is born of forgiven sin that has something unique and special in its flavour, and which has a special place in God's plan. Past sins, past failures, need never come between us and Him; provided we are truly contrite, they only make a new bond. So also, fears for the future, and that lack of full goodwill that comes from human weakness and timidity, need never be anything but a new claim on the help of Him who came to heal the sick and to save sinners. His official position in our soul is that of an omnipotent Saviour; all that needs saving is a claim on Him, and only those who have learned to glory in their infirmities know to the full how intimate a union of prayer and work with Jesus can be built on their own weakness, on their own failures, and even on their past sins.

This is also true of our sharing in His cross. He knows well our horror of penance; He understands perfectly our dislike of suffering; nay, more, He sympathises with us in these difficulties. True, He wishes us to help Him to carry His cross, but He also wishes to help us to do so. So sweet is His aid, so enthralling His companionship, that St. Teresa found that it was only the first of her crosses that was really hard; once she had embraced the nettle of her cross she found herself in close union with Jesus. There is no joy in this life to equal that of sharing the cross with Jesus. It needs courage, it needs grace, it needs perhaps a special call; but the truth is that this path of suffering and of penance—penance, be it well understood, undertaken or accepted according to God's will and not our own—is the road of highest joy, and the sure path to the heights of prayer.

The importance of mortification is not so much that it hurts us, but that it gives Jesus a new life in us; we only put ourselves to death—that is what "mortification" means—in order to clear the way for Christ. That is at once the motive of mortification and its measure. If it only serves to make us more self-satisfied and proud, then it is no longer mortification of self; it is rather the mortification of Jesus. The true principle of mortification was laid down by St. John the Baptist when he said: "He must increase, I must decrease."

Perhaps a somewhat far-fetched comparison may help to put this process in its true light. The bread and wine that are changed into the Body and Blood of Our Lord at Mass once graced the earth in a glory of purple and gold; they were cut down, beaten and bruised, ground and pressed out of all recognition. Not until many changes had been made in them could the priest say over them the words that would make them the Flesh and Blood of Christ. Now, in so far as the Mass is a changing of bread and wine into the Body and Blood of Jesus—it is, of course, much more than that—it might be said that Our Lord says Mass with us and our lives as the bread and wine, but it is a Mass in which the grinding of the wheat and the pressing of the grape, the baking of the bread and the maturing of the wine, the offering of the Host and the oblation of the

Chalice, the consecration of both and their conversion into the living Body and Blood of Christ, are all going on at the same time. Every time that we deny ourselves in any way and to that extent offer ourselves to Jesus, He comes and takes possession of us to that same extent, and says: "This is My Body." More than that: He takes compassion on our cowardice, and sends us trials and humiliations that grind us and press us and make us into suitable bread and wine to become part of Himself. "My meat," He said, "is to do the will of Him that sent Me." So it is that everything done in accordance with the Divine will gives new life to Jesus in our souls, for He feeds on the doing of His Father's will. Every action we do, every suffering we undergo, whatever it be, as long as it is according to the will of God, is an act of communion with Jesus, an act that is no mere desire, but a positive advance in our union with Him; it gives Him new matter over which He can pronounce the saving words: "This is My Body."

The significance of such a concept for a life of prayer is obvious. Prayer is no longer a matter of some few minutes spent on our knees, struggling to find something to say. It becomes a more or less continual awareness of Jesus living in us, of Jesus growing in us, of Jesus moulding us by His providence to His Heart's desire; our co-operation, our companionship, our submission, our smile of surrender as we continually give up our own way in order to let Him have His way—all these are our prayer. Mortification, instead of meaning doing hurt to ourselves, comes to mean giving pleasure, giving even life, to Jesus. Every action of the day is intimately concerned with Him.

The practice of Christian charity is thus put in a stronger light, for if Jesus lives in our neighbour, and is making our neighbour's life His own, it becomes much easier to realise what He meant when He told us : "As often as you did it to the least of these, My brethren, you did it to Me." To turn our dealings with our fellow-men into prayer, we have no need of words. It is sufficient to remember that "we are doing it to Him," and our heart will pray by its secret movement of love. The practice of one of the greatest men of prayer and of action that the world has seen—one who comes very close to St. Paul—is full of meaning in this matter. St. Patrick's mind is given to us in his famous "Breastplate," that wonderful prayer, full of the spirit of St. Paul, full of the spirit of Christ Himself. "Christ before me," he prays, "Christ behind me, Christ about me, Christ be this day within and without me, Christ the lowly and meek, Christ the all-powerful, be in the heart of each one to whom I speak—in the mouth of each who speaks to me, in all who draw near me, or see or hear me." He tells us of how he heard the words: "He Who laid down His life for thee—He it is that prayeth in thee." On another occasion he writes: "I saw Him praying in me," and on being told that it was the Spirit who prayeth within him, he recalls St. Paul's promise that the Holy Ghost should help the infirmities of our prayer. We have here the secret of St. Patrick's prayer, the secret of his interior life and, in fact, the secret of the monumental success of his active life—union with God in his own soul, and the service of God in the soul of his neighbour. There is no Christian who cannot imitate that example.

CHAPTER SEVENTEEN

EMMANUEL— "GOD WITH US"

The example of St. Patrick, and the insight that the few words just quoted from his writings give us into his heart, show us the secret of the wonderful way in which many of the saints were able to unite a life of prayer with a life of almost continual action. All our activity can be reduced either to the service of Christ in our neighbour, or to the extending of His life in ourselves. It will have been noted that the border-line between prayer, in the usual association of the term, and the rest of one's activities, is gradually being removed as we progress in the consideration of the spiritual life. And that is as it should be, for Our Lord Himself told us that we ought always to pray. But it must not be concluded from this that there is no need of some time during the day in which we are to devote our undivided attention to prayer. For, as we have seen, although all our acts can be prayer, they will not be so unless there are some acts which are nothing else. That is to say: human nature is such that if the interior life is not fed by reflection and by pure prayer, it will gradually succumb to the lure of natural activity that will soon take complete charge of our actions. In fact, even under the most favourable conditions, the habitual remembrance of Our Lord can only be developed after repeated failures. But once it has been achieved, even to a somewhat limited extent, the whole spiritual life undergoes a remarkable transformation. In many ways it becomes easier and more attractive.

The thought of mortification and war on self fills many souls with fear, and causes them to turn back and give up the hope of further progress. This is quite understandable, but it is also quite foolish, for Our Lord Himself has said that His yoke is easy and His burden light. Mortification is like some of those old houses on the Continent, which are grim and forbidding barrack-like structures from the outside, but contain inside a courtyard filled with all the glamour of a southern garden, echoing with the music of falling fountains, and fragrant with the rich odour of flowers. We have looked through those grim gates and have seen that what seems to be the living death of mortification is in reality the growth of Jesus in our soul, filling us with the warmth of His smile, the melody of His companionship, and the glow of His love. For by dying to ourselves we have given Him a new measure of life.

In considering this mystery of the life and growth of Jesus in our souls and our incorporation in Him, we have looked at it from a number of different points of view. It can be regarded as the indwelling in our soul of the Holy Ghost, who, somewhat after the fashion of the soul in the human body which makes one thing, one body, one person of many members, makes all of us into one thing, one Body, and even as we may say in a real but limited sense, one Person—one Christ. Or we can regard this mystery as our own incorporation into Christ after the manner of a grafting of a branch on to a new stem; we have Our Lord's own authority for claiming that we ourselves are branches of the Vine that He identified with Himself. Then, too, we can look upon the mystery as the dwelling in our soul of Jesus Himself in a wonderful union of saving co-operation and living love; for this we have the authority of His own promises. At first sight we may think that we have thus involved ourselves in a contradiction through making use of all these different views; but that is only because the richness of this mystery, which involves a reality without any parallel in the whole of creation, is such as to demand many different analogies for its expression. Despite this difficulty, and despite the frequent use of the word "mystical" to describe it, we must never doubt its reality. It is the greatest of all realities outside God: it is our only hope, it is the plan of God, who wills to restore all things "in Christ."

At the risk of adding to the confusion which this manifold exposition may seem to involve, it would be well to indicate another way of regarding the mystery, because it may be of help to some souls in their prayer. Our Lord, taking a human body in the womb of His Mother Mary, became man, lived His own human life for our salvation, and died and rose again for that same end. Not that that was His sole end, for the glory of the Father must have come before all else. But He wished to glorify His Father's mercy by saving us. Now, this process did not end with the Resurrection. Risen from the dead, He continues His life in each one of us. We might look upon the whole stretch of our existence as if it were a body—a body without animation, for without Christ it is supernaturally dead—a body into which Christ is gradually being born, according as through the operations of grace and the co-operation of our own will, we gradually submit more and more of our actions to Him.

This concept has to some extent the authority of St. Paul who tells the Galatians that He is "in labour" until Christ be formed in them. We, too, are "in labour" till Christ be formed in ourselves. This is a view that it is important not to overlook. But it is still more important to attend to the significance of Our Lord's words to His Mother and to St. John as He poured out the last drops of His lifeblood on the Cross at Calvary: "Behold thy son—Behold thy Mother." St. John there stood for the whole human race. Mary is thus shown to be the Mother of each of us, being given, as it were, the life of the dying Christ that She might transmit it to us. A certain measure of caution is here necessary to prevent too close a degree of identification between the life of Jesus in His own Flesh and that which He lives in us. Still, the Encyclical Letter of Pope Pius X, *Ad diem ilium*, published on 2nd February, 1904, shows us that we can carry this notion of the maternity of Mary in reference to ourselves very far, without departing from his teaching or making any innovation, for the Holy Father quotes the very words of St. Augustine in support of this doctrine. The Pope asserts not only that it was in Mary that Christ took to Himself flesh, but also that in Mary He united to Himself the spiritual body formed by those who are to believe in Him.

Here, then, is a view that may give Our Lady a new importance in our spiritual life and a new significance for our prayer. She is not only the Mother of Christ, but she is also really and actively mother to each of us who believe in Him. She was instrumental in uniting the human nature of Christ to the Word; she is also instrumental in uniting each of us to Christ—for we are His Body.

Mary is continually co-operating in the formation of Christ in us, so much so that we could say that He is continually being born in us of her. Every time we submit any part of our life to God by doing His will in the way in which He wills, she brings forth in our soul a new measure of the fullness of Christ, and we co-operate in her maternity.

Thus, the spiritual life is not only lived in union with the Blessed Trinity, but it is also an active union with Mary. Here it may be noted that all that has been said in an earlier chapter on the value of the familiar friendship with Jesus as a way of developing a life of prayer, also applies, *mutatis mutandis*, to a filial familiarity with Mary. Nor need it be thought that to seek God by recourse to Mary is to lose time by following a roundabout path. Not only is there no time lost, but it would seem that to go to Him through Mary is not only the shorter, but also the surer way. she is the way chosen by God to come to us. By her intercession she can do all that God can do by His power; she is only too glad to use every opportunity of doing something more for Her Child Jesus, and she knows better than anyone else how true it is that all that is done to the least of us is done to Him. These considerations may encourage those souls who find themselves more at their ease in talking to Mary than in any other way of praying. They may rest assured that she will leave nothing undone to unite them to Jesus, nor will the attention they pay to her derogate in the slightest from that due to her Son. It is, of course, true that Mary is not present within us in the same way as is her Son, but her function as Mother, both in our regard and in that of Christ, ensures that her hand is always near and able to help us. Her ears are quick to hear us, and her eyes never lose sight of us. Our prayers need no words to carry them to her ears; the mere smile of our heart, the sigh of our soul, are seen by her immediately, and there need be no delay before she is come to our help. She is the Refuge of sinners, the Comforter of the afflicted; she is the Mother of Perpetual Succour, the Mother of Divine Grace; she is the Mother of Christ and of us all. There is no one who need be afraid to speak to her of his needs, there is no one whose needs are beyond her powers, there is no one whose sins will turn her away from him. There is no work, save that of sin, that may not be done under her eyes, and the true picture of the spiritual life lived in union with Mary is that of a child at work or at play, secure in the consciousness of his mother seated within call, always ready to take an interest in his doings and never unable to help.

CHAPTER EIGHTEEN

ASSETS AND LIABILITIES

In the last few chapters an attempt was made to sketch in the merest outline some of the wonders which God has wrought in the soul of every Christian. To treat the subject properly, even were it only in its relation to a life of prayer, would require many long chapters. It must here suffice to point out the rich mine that the subject forms, and hope that the reader will seek elsewhere for its development. The Epistles of St. Paul are, of course, a primary source. The many fine works that have appeared in recent times on the Mystical Body of Christ will throw much new light on the question. The works of Mura, of Anger, of Mersch, of Sheen, are already classics on this subject. The works of Fr. de Jaegher, of Fr. Plus, of Fr. Duperray, are only some of the many smaller books which apply the doctrine to the spiritual life. Dom Marmion's writings have already made an everlasting place for themselves in spiritual literature. There is no need to develop the theme here any further.

To sum up, then: in Baptism Christ makes each of us a member of Himself; He gives us His Father by making us sons of God; He gives us His Mother, as we have just seen, to be our Mother also. He gives us His own Spirit to vivify us with the newness and fullness of life. He gives us His own life, in so far as He died for us and rose again for us and comes to live His life in us. He gives us His merits, for we can truly call them our own. He gives us His innocence, for He has taken our sins upon Himself. He gives us His Flesh and

Blood for our nourishment that we may live by Him. He gives us Himself, uniting us to Himself, in such a way that without losing our own personality, we "put on Christ," and can live and act and pray in His Name as indeed He lives and acts and prays in our name. So close is the union, so time-defying, that every sin we commit adds to His Passion—every cross we patiently bear lightens His own. Our love comforts Him in the Garden, just as our neglect or disloyalty makes Him suffer even to the sweating of Blood. So complete is this union that each of us can say in the words of St. Paul: "And I live, now not I: but Christ liveth in me."

It must be remembered that these truths do not apply merely to a select and mystical few; they are the primary facts of Christianity, and are true of every baptized person. Baptism is not merely the removal of original sin, it is also the infusion of a new life. The chief obstacles to this life in us are the desires of the flesh, the desires of the eyes, and the pride of life. Now, the three vows that constitute the religious state, those of poverty, chastity and obedience, are directly aimed at destroying these obstacles and in making full room for Christ in our lives, or rather for His life in us. What religious then can say that holiness is not for him? What right has any religious to maintain that he is not called to a life of prayer? How can a religious believe that God does not intend *him* to go beyond the very first step of the ladder of prayer? And even if special graces are necessary for the heights of prayer, how can a religious, who by his state is already bound to all that he needs do to prepare himself for these graces—to whom God has already given Himself, His Son, and His Spirit—how can he refuse to hope that God will give him all that is necessary to live a life of union with His Son? If we have received so much from God, why may we not hope for what—in comparison at least—is only a little more, especially when we have already received the right to ask in the name of His Son? The very question suggests its own answer, for the only reason for fearing a refusal is that we are not really asking in the name of Jesus. If, however, we are living in the name of Jesus, if, at least, we are doing our best to do so, if we are come so far as to want Him to live in us still more and more, and if we see that these graces of prayer are the very means to extend His life in ours, then let us ask in all confidence, nothing doubting.

Before we go on to consider further progress in prayer, let us look back for a moment on the road we are travelling. In the beginning, if by education and environment we had not already been familiarised with the convictions of faith, we prayed by "meditation." That is, we recalled some truth, and applied our intellect to consider different points in it, illustrating it by pictures in our imagination; we deduced certain conclusions, and set our will to work in resolutions and turned all our faculties to God in a colloquy or short conversation. These convictions became habitual as time went on, the idea of God became more familiar to us; in particular, our imagination had no great difficulty in forming a very real picture of Our Lord, and we found that it became more easy to talk to Him, so much so that when we went to prayer we had no need of long considerations to find something to say to Him. As the books say, the affections predominated in our prayer. This association with Our Lord ripened into friendship, and our mutual understanding became so great that a few words sufficed for our conversation, and sometimes we could even do without words altogether, and were content to kneel in silent adoration or wordless desire. Our prayer simplified itself. Granting the essentially supernatural condition of all prayer and its consequent dependence on grace, this progress may be described as a natural one. It is only what may be expected, if we do not fail to make our life accord with our friendship with Jesus. Provided we were loyal to Him, and were careful that our actions were in harmony with His ideals and in particular with the requests He made of us, intimate understanding and silent communion followed quite naturally. The same conditions are required for human friendship, and a similar result may be expected when they are realised.

Still, there were many "ups-and-downs" in our progress. Each falling off in virtue was reflected by a corresponding failure in prayer. Distractions were always a threat to our prayer and often almost destroyed it. In some cases, too, the growth in simplicity was obscured by a constant habit of vocal prayer, or perhaps by a vigorous devotion to methodic meditation. This latter, if pressed too far, is by no means the best way to the heights of prayer, although it can be a fine foundation; but God is faithful, and His grace is all-powerful. As the proverb puts it, He can write straight on crooked lines.

Despite all the trials and the troubles, however, there were, perhaps, times when we tasted the sweetness of the friendship of Jesus.
There were times when prayer simply flowed from our lips, when
our heart glowed with devotion, when we felt ready for any sacrifice.
We could *feel* our prayer. Then, perhaps, this sensible devotion, for
such it was, in part at least, grew less. The mysteries of Jesus failed
to touch us in the same way, the supernatural lost its appeal for us,
and prayer became an arid dreary business of banishing distractions and having nothing to put in their place. Our "devotion" was
dead, and it was hard to know what to do next. Innate conviction of
a world to come kept us on the straight path, and we plunged into
our work with as much earnestness as we could muster. A life of
prayer was not for us—we were not called to serve God in that fashion. So, perhaps, it seemed to some. Were they right?

First of all, this development just sketched could be merely natural. It was founded on grace, of course, but still it might have been
no more than what might be called the "natural" working of grace-
aided nature. Actually, although the nature of things would be sufficient explanation, it does often happen that Our Lord Himself
intervenes in the natural progress, and does so to accelerate and
extend our advance. His way of doing so, however, is what should
be noticed, for, in its later stages at any rate, it runs quite contrary
to what one would expect. In the earlier stages, He frequently does
act in a special way to intensify sensible devotion; He even makes
His presence felt, and touches our hearts so sweetly that, for the
moment at any rate, we make great advances in detachment. But in
our reaction to these favours there is a lot of self-love—"cupboard
love," as the old people used to call it—and, in any case, the senses
cannot bring us far on our road to God. True, these favours help to
set us on the road, but they are not real devotion—they do not supply the motive-power for a long and tedious journey. Real devotion
is in the will, in a determination to follow Christ, cost us what it may.
That is the only sort of devotion that will keep us advancing on the
narrow way that leads to the Kingdom of God.

Our Lord, therefore, once He has turned our hearts to Himself,
begins to purify our love and our devotion. Sooner or later He
begins to withdraw this sensible devotion, and our prayer runs
"dry." We tend to become sullen and resentful; but if we are generous and try to co-operate with His grace, we shall soon see that what

He wants from us is complete and generous submission to His will. That is all that matters, and we must learn to find all our satisfaction in doing that. That calls for courage; it calls for faith; it calls for grace. It is as expedient for us that He go away as it was for the Apostles; otherwise we should continue to live by our senses rather than by generous faith. Now, the senses cannot unite us to God in any full meaning of the word; it is in faith that Our Lord espouses us to Himself, and until we have learned to live by faith, we are but novices in the spiritual life, no matter to what heights of sensible devotion we have risen. The natural blunting of sense reaction that comes from familiarity with, and repetition of, the same experience—the unconscious realisation, if one may so speak, of the inadequacy of any feeling or emotion to satisfy the deeper needs of our soul—these, added to the workings of God's purifications, bring us to a new phase of the spiritual life, where prayer becomes a matter of great difficulty. Although it is usually in the later stages of the spiritual ascent that this state is found in long and constant duration—for it may last for many years—yet it often occurs much earlier for shorter periods, and it is only when we have estimated it at its proper worth that we can form any true scale of values of prayer. For such a state, in spite of its apparent sterility and worthlessness, leads to a prayer of tremendous value, one most pleasing to God and most productive of great virtue and rapid advance for ourselves. It is a state in which one has to love and pray by faith, and for that reason the term "prayer of faith" is used here to denote this type of prayer.

CHAPTER NINETEEN

THE PRAYER
OF FAITH

U nder the term "prayer of faith" are here included all those forms of prayer in which neither the senses nor the intellect find much to hold them or attract their natural appetites. This prayer centres rather around God as seen by the dim light of faith, with His attractiveness dimmed and hidden. It is a prayer which seems to consist in an inability to pray. It is not to our purpose, however, to narrow down the meaning of the name by trying to define it. On the contrary, it is better to leave its application as broad as possible, so as to be able to include in the treatment of it the permanent difficulties of the more advanced as well as the temporary paralysis of those who have not yet got so far.

Many readers do not like quotations, but one feels bound to quote the description given by St. Jane Francis de Chantal of her prayer, both because it is an excellent, though advanced, example of the type of prayer that is under discussion, and also because it may introduce that saint to some who have not yet known her. After St. Teresa, she is the great authority of her sex on prayer. She is, moreover, the living book that St. Francis de Sales "wrote," for he was her director and formed her soul on the lines of his now classic spirituality—a spirituality that has hardly ever been surpassed.

The saint writes: "I tell you in all confidence and simplicity that it is about twenty years since God took from me all power to accomplish anything in prayer with the understanding and consideration or meditation; and that all I can do is to suffer and stay my spirit very simply in God, cleaving to this operation by an entire committal (or abandonment to God) without making any acts, unless I should be invited thereto by His motion, there awaiting what it shall please His goodness to give me." Here we have a prayer without "acts," without ability to do anything except to suffer and to abandon one's self to God. It is this latter point that distinguishes this prayer from mere reveries or lazy inertness. If one's life is not being continually moulded according to God's will, there can be no real "abandonment" at the time of prayer. The note of suffering is not essential to this prayer, but all the same, prayer frequently fails because we do not regard it as a means by which we give ourselves to God. Too often we are seeking consolations, seeking ourselves, in fact, even though it be on a spiritual plane. We are praying in our own name, instead of that of Jesus Christ.

There are various phases of prayer which can be included under this title "prayer of faith." Sometimes we cannot conceive that God is anywhere near us. He seems to have abandoned us completely, to be indifferent to our needs. Nothing we can say or do seems to move Him. At other times, it is our own efforts that seem to be at fault. We cannot form a single act. Words die on our lips as soon as they are born; they are completely inadequate. We want something: what it is we cannot say. We can only, as it were, whimper or moan. Sometimes an acute consciousness of our misery kills our prayer, as, for example, when our protestations of love are choked by the remembrance of our daily infidelity, of our self-seeking, or of our lack of trust.

It may be, perhaps, that we are conscious in some blind way that God is not far away; He seems to be behind a heavy thick curtain in complete darkness. But every effort we make to draw near to Him or to speak to Him only seems to put us further away from Him. It is like a man swimming who raises himself up over the water to try and see farther, only to fall back even lower again. Sometimes we are, so to speak, in touch with God, but are beset with distractions, and every effort to get rid of these distractions only serves to break our contact with God. This is a state, referred to by St. Teresa, in which no attempt should be made to banish the distractions. It is somewhat analogous to the case of a hostess entertaining a visitor on the ground floor while her children are making noise upstairs. If she goes up to keep them quiet, she has to leave her visitor. In this particular phase of prayer, God's action is confined to the very depth of the soul, and makes no appeal to the senses or to the imagination, nor does He offer the intellect anything of which it can lay hold with ease. These powers then start to work on their own, and any attempt to follow them will only take the soul away from God.

This, however, is but a particular case. In all these cases where one is helpless, incurably distracted, paralysed by dryness, completely unable to get into touch with God, apparently quite indifferent to all the things of God, even at times filled with distaste for them, or beset with stupidity, vacancy of mind, and even temptations—in all such cases one has to fall back on a "dry" act of faith in God, in His presence, in His power, in His goodness, in His knowledge, in His infinite mercy, and in His Fatherly love. This state of prayer consists not so much in one long uninterrupted act as in an habitual permanent disposition to avoid whatever displeases God and to perform whatever pleases Him. Be it noted that this fundamental disposition is quite consistent with a general feeling of sinfulness and of apparent bad-will. It only ceases when we become aware of a particular deliberate determination to persevere in something contrary to the will of God. This, of course, is the end of our good-will. But, given this good-will, we can apply to our prayer the principle found in the prayer of the Church when she thus addresses God: "O God, to whom every heart lies open and to whom we speak with our wills. . . ." We must, therefore, pray with our wills.

We pray with our will whenever we go to prayer, in accordance with God's will, and put ourselves in a suitable attitude of body, turning our mind, as far as we can, away from all else but God, and endeavouring to persevere in that attitude of mind and body. This is true, no matter how often we are distracted, no matter how little we say, no matter how remote from God we feel, no matter how much we seem to have failed; for, nevertheless, we have been praying with our will. And that is all that matters. We may have got absolutely no satisfaction out of such prayer, but God has been duly honoured, and be it noted, we ourselves, though we know it not, have been made more holy and more pleasing to God. If souls could only realise the value of this sort of prayer, what new courage they would feel! For it is the idea that all our time is wasted in such an attempt that makes us give up prayer when it develops into the sort of state that we have been trying to describe.

It is in order that they may have a true notion of what progress in prayer really means that this description is put before the eyes of all, even those beginning the spiritual life. The ordinary notion of progress is something quite opposed to developments of this sort. Yet the ordinary notion is wrong, for it judges prayer by the self-satisfaction that it affords. This is a false criterion, for prayer's purpose is to give God His due, not to yield us that to which we have no right. If God is pleased that we should stand before Him like dumb animals or like a statue, is it not meet and just, and right and fitting that we should do so? But then we shall have to learn to find our happiness in pleasing God, not in pleasing ourselves.

In other words, we must make our life "Christ-centred" instead of self-centred. Then we shall be satisfied by the hope that the dreary minutes we spend in prayer will lighten His cross. Very often, if we would but make up our mind to share His cross, we should rediscover Our Divine Lover, Who seems to have abandoned us. However, that is not always the case. He may still remain far away, despite our generosity in sacrifice, and we shall have to be content to serve Him at our own expense until He sees fit to come again to set our hearts on fire.

That He will come again if we persevere in prayer is certain, for this arid stage is but the desert that guards the approach to the promised land of contemplation. There is indeed a very close parallel between the progress of the soul when this paralysis in prayer has become a permanent condition and the wanderings of the Israelites in the desert. Despite everything, there is, deep down in the soul, a vague habitual hunger for something that it may or may not recognise to be God. Nothing in creation can give it solid satisfaction; and even though it may sigh for the joys it previously knew in the spiritual life, it knows in the depths of its heart that these can no longer satisfy its needs. It has left Egypt and its fleshpots; it has not yet reached the promised land; meanwhile, it must learn to content itself with the daily manna God gives it. Nor will it receive more than a day's supply, for God only gives the soul enough grace to meet the needs of the moment, so that it may learn that of itself it can do nothing, but that His grace is always sufficient for it.

When a soul in this condition feels itself moved to kneel before God, doing nothing, except, in a general way, waiting for Him, there need be no doubt that it is really praying and, in fact, that God is preparing it for further graces of prayer. This state, which is called the dark night of the senses, is by no means so unusual as many suppose. The soul in this state is in need of more counsel than can be given here. There are two small books which treat of this condition in a very practical way, and which can be recommended to all souls who are trying to live a life of prayer. One is *On Prayer*, by Fr. de Caussade, S.J.; the other is *The Science of Prayer*, by Father Ludovic de Besse, O.S.F.Cap. (This latter at the moment is, unfortunately, out of print.) The matter treated in these two books should be familiar to every priest and religious of five or six years' standing. Both books treat of the simplified types of prayer and of the difficulties and doubts that arise from them, and discuss many other aspects of the spiritual life connected with this stage of prayer. The reader will find great encouragement in their pages, and will get much help to persevere in prayer, despite its obscurities and aridities. Even the beginner will be encouraged to dispose himself for progress by generous efforts.

The works of St. Teresa should be read, for she may be called an official teacher of prayer in light of the collect said in her Mass. Nor is she without sympathy for, or experience of, the weaknesses and repugnances of human nature. St. John of the Cross frightens many who do not know him, but two of his works, *The Ascent of Mount Carmel* and *The Dark Night of the Soul*, will be of great help to many who have false notions of prayer. He it was who gave the Little Flower such light and encouragement. *The Spiritual Life*, by Tanquerey, is, as already noted, an invaluable work of reference on this as on all questions of the spiritual life. There are two large works on prayer that can be read with profit: *The Graces of Interior Prayer*, by Father Poulain, S.J., and *The Degrees of the Spiritual Life*, by Canon Saudreau. These two writers represent different schools of thought, but both agree in putting the higher stages of prayer before us as something to be desired and prayed for, and something for which we should dispose ourselves. The part of Fr. Poulain's work which treats of the prayer of simplicity has been reprinted in pamphlet form by the English C.T.S., but his treatment of what he terms the prayer of quiet should also be read. Reference has already been made to *Holy Wisdom*, by Fr. Augustine Baker, O.S.B.; *A Book of Spiritual Instruction*, by Blosius, is a classic of the same school. The work of Dom Vital Lehodey, O.C.R., *The Ways of Mental Prayer*, is admitted to be one of the best practical handbooks on the subject; while a little book by Dom Chautard, O.C.R., *The Soul of the Apostolate*, is a most readable and effective summing-up of the absolute need for an interior life in all forms of spiritual activity.

But knowledge alone is not enough. The three infused theological virtues of faith, hope, and charity are of ever-increasing importance in the life of prayer. It is, however, the need of faith that demands to be stressed here—of faith, not merely during the act of praying, but also during the whole spiritual life, for, as we have seen, prayer becomes more and more closely connected with the rest of the spiritual life as it progresses. From one point of view, all progress and purification in this matter might be roughly summed up as a gradual replacement of seeing, feeling, and perceiving—by believing. For the sensual man—whom we can here take to be the man who lives by feeling and the senses—perceiveth not the tilings of God. The just man, as St. Paul tells us, lives by faith. Sooner or later the soul who would come close to God must live by a naked faith, believing in the midst of darkness by a sheer effort of the grace-aided will. One might even say that the soul will have to "believe" in its own fervour; it certainly will not be able to "feel" it.

Without faith, no one would think of entering religion; without faith, no one would value the Sacraments; without faith, no one would give supernatural obedience to a fallible human superior. The whole of religious obedience rests on faith, and this a faith that may have to be exercised in the teeth of the opposition caused by the spirit of human independence in the subject, or by apparent human weakness in the superior, for even if the superior is a saint in all his works, our own human eye will manage to find some failing in his words or reasons—something that arouses our opposition and tempts us to cry out: "I will not serve"—something that can only be overcome by the faith that sees God's hand and will in all the official works of His appointed representatives.

St. Thomas Aquinas tells us that it is by the two channels of faith and of the Sacraments that the Passion of Christ is applied to our souls. Faith is demanded by the Church for Baptism. Faith is required from us by Our Lord when we pray. Faith is the breath of the spiritual life, the substance of things hoped for, the evidence of things that appear not. The importance, then, of living by faith, even in the early stages of the spiritual life, is evident. "Without faith it is impossible to please God." And since progress will only lead us to a life of pure faith, the more we try to live by faith, the sooner and the more rapidly shall we advance.

In one connection faith is of capital importance, that is, in the reception of the Sacraments, and, in particular, immediately before their reception. Although the Sacraments have their own power of action, yet the extent of the grace they produce in us depends very much on our dispositions, in particular on our faith, hope, and charity. By stirring up our faith, we lay the foundation for an increase of hope and charity, and thus promote our rapid growth in the spiritual life.

But the chief importance of faith is that it is faith that unites us to God in this life. Neither our senses nor our reason can lay hold of God, but faith touches God and keeps us in a vital contact with Him that makes us one with Him. The use of our senses and reason can even become an obstacle to this union, and so St. John of the Cross insists that all these faculties must be completely mortified, and the soul must learn to live by faith alone, before it can be completely united to God. Since union with God is the essence of the whole spiritual life, the supreme importance of faith in every phase of that life is evident; above all, it is indispensable for prayer.

CHAPTER TWENTY

"MANY ARE CALLED ..."

T here is a further reason which makes it advisable for the soul trying to live a life of prayer to consult the literature of the subject. We have been watching its progress after its departure from the fleshpots of Egypt, following it through the desert of dry and arid prayer, where it has to learn to live by the manna of faith. It is not to our purpose to discuss its further progress; but since we are on the borders of the Promised Land, one must beware lest one commit the original fault of leaving the soul under a wrong and gloomy impression about the great joys that await it in that land flowing with milk and honey. Still, one cannot here attempt to describe the delights and consolations of the different sorts of contemplative prayer that may be granted to the soul who has been courageous enough to trust in God's guidance and persevere in following Him through the desert of darkness. The literature already indicated, or such first-hand accounts as are found, say, in the life of St. Teresa, will help the soul to realise that a foretaste of heaven on this earth lies before it.

It is true that, although the soul's trials are by no means over when it nears the summit of the mountain of prayer, there are no joys in this life to equal those that the heights of prayer can bring. Whether all are called to this high state or not is a question that need not detain us. It is, however, quite safe to say that all may laudably pray and prepare themselves for the higher graces of prayer, provided that their motives are sound and that they base their hope on the mercy of God, on the merits of Our Saviour, and on their own

poverty of spirit. In thus working towards the graces of prayer, nothing is lost, for, as we have pointed out, the work of preparation is
nothing else but the generous accomplishment of all that is already
required by the nature of the religious state or by the office of the
priesthood. Of course, the condition of the soul for which God normally waits before He bestows His graces of contemplative prayer in
any high degree, implies no small measure of self-abnegation and
virtue.

But God is no respecter of persons, and for His own wise ends
He often bestows His grace—even His special grace—where there
is little or no merit. Besides, even when He does wait for a stable
state of generous service before calling the soul to a higher place at
the banquet of His love, He Himself is the most earnest and the
most energetic agent in the work of the soul's preparation.

In any case, this level of fervour is no higher than that which can
be, and which really should be, attained in the religious life. The
tragedy is that so many souls go far on the way to attain this state
and make nearly all the necessary sacrifices, but let themselves be
prevented from finishing their course by an attachment to some
tawdry trifle that they will not try to give up. If, in fact, a number of
priests and of souls in religion do fail to reach contemplation, it is
not so much that too high a degree of perfection is required for its
attainment, but rather because of some obstinate refusal on their
part to deny some small desire of self-love. "The little more, and oh!
how much!" From the moment that we deliberately decide to persist in a refusal of some request that we know God is making of us,
that self-surrender which is the foundation of our union with God
is destroyed, and contemplative prayer, which is the flower and fruit
of that union, is quite out of the question. Sometimes it is the very
gift of God that we refuse to give up, holding on to His consolations
like a child that refuses to be weaned. We forget the exhortation of
the Apostles to be zealous for better gifts; we forget the great principle "Trade till I come," for we must always use the gifts of God in
trading with Him and on His mercy, until He gives us Himself in as
close a union as possible. That is why generosity and a spirit of self-
sacrifice are so essential for advance in prayer. We must give God a
blank cheque on ourselves and on all that we have, relying on His
grace and mercy to give us all the means to meet each of His
requests for payment in surrender and in sacrifice.

In this connection, it may be said that if anyone try the experiment, if one may call it such, of refusing God nothing for a period, say, of six months, he will be amazed at the transformation in his spiritual life. If we only had the courage to abandon ourselves to Him whom we know with such certainty to be so loving a Father! If we only could stir up our faith and realise that Our Lord meant what He said—that His yoke *is* easy and His burden light! Is it not extraordinary that we cannot take God at His word?

To reach such heights of prayer is impossible without a resolute spirit of mortification. Deliberate habits of sin must be absolutely renounced and vigorously resisted. The deliberate and habitual breach of any rule, of any command of superiors, or a similar neglect of any duty, has to be eliminated also. Further, we must never allow a spirit of self-indulgence to take charge of our conduct; our guiding spirit should be one of self-sacrifice. At first sight this seems hard—too hard—but it becomes lighter and more "reasonable" when we realise that we are only asked to mortify ourselves in order that Jesus may live in us. Our death to ourselves by mortification is His resurrection in us, and so we must learn to try in all eventualities to act for the sake of Jesus rather than for love of our own ease. That means that we must declare war on our self-seeking, and make it our constant aim to seek Jesus. It further means that we must try to accept cheerfully all the trials that He sends us, of whatever sort they be—trials of soul, trials of body, trials from within, trials from without, trials from men, trials from work—and to see in them a new chance of uniting ourselves to Jesus in suffering, of lightening His cross, and of filling up what is wanting for the Church in the sufferings of Christ. They will serve as another occasion of uniting ourselves in faith to our loving Father, who rules all things sweetly and makes all work together for our good. They will also be an occasion of uniting ourselves to the Holy Spirit, who dwells in us to give strength to our weakness and light to our blindness, so that we may meet the needs of every moment.

But does a spirit of mortification mean any more than that? Does it mean, perhaps, that we must undertake a programme of penance—particularly of corporal penance? This is a somewhat delicate question, because the answer depends considerably on particular circumstances. It is undoubtedly true that if men did more penance, there would be many more raised to the prayer of true contemplation. On the other hand, indiscreet and imprudent attempts at inflicting penance upon one's self have more than once led to disaster. The motives and the effect must be healthy, and the matter is one in which the individual is not a competent judge of his own case. In the more penitential orders, the customary measure of mortification practised by fervent souls should never be exceeded without competent advice, and even then should be controlled by some prudent authority, even if that can only be done at long intervals. In those orders that do not provide for much penance in their regular life, and also in the life of the clergy, there is obviously more room, and even need, for personal initiative. Again, however, one cannot give a general dispensation from the time-proved need for advice and control, though one must admit the difficulty—which is in some cases almost an impossibility—of finding a prudent and competent adviser who has the leisure and the inclination for the direction of souls. Yet God's providence must have provided for these cases, and fervour added to prayer will always find the right person. In general, it may be said that those fasts in which our own will is found have excellent authority for their reprobation. Those penances that interfere with the proper performance of the duties of our state are by that very fact condemned. Those that we can do with a "dry" but genuine cheerfulness and that do not pre-occupy us too much, nor puff us up and make us thank God that we are not like the rest of men—all such are salutary and sound. Penance should be done in a spirit of compunction, to atone for our sins, but, better still, it should also be done in union with Our Lord, to lighten the load of His cross and to fulfil the fellowship of His love and suffering.

If one here tried to summarise the conditions that are required for contemplation, one would be compelled to write at great length, for it would mean making a complete summary of the perfection of the spiritual life. But it must be insisted, that if one did so, one would not have to mention a single disposition or achievement which every religious, active as well as contemplative, is not already bound to seek by the obligations of his state, or else expected to acquire for its perfection. And, as we have seen, the office of the priesthood makes similar demands on its holders. The tragedy is that there are so many priests and religious who have "kept all these things from their youth," and then, when Our Lord draws their attention to some attachment that He wants them to give up, who turn away sorrowful—for they think they have many possessions— many talents—many dreams—many hopes, too much to give up. And the thing that holds them is so tawdry and so trifling, is so trag- ically trash, that the angels must stare in amazement that men can be so mad.

Whole-hearted fidelity to God's will in the faithful following of His commandments, in the exact observance of one's rules, of one's daily duties, of the exercise of the common life; generosity in corre- sponding with the inspirations of grace, in determining to refuse God nothing that He clearly asks for, in abandoning one's self to every detail of His providence; humility which distrusts its own strength, and puts all its confidence in God's merciful help alone; a resolute desire of fulfilling every detail of God's requirements— these will lead a soul to advance quickly and beyond all expecta- tions. A soul so minded will soon find that God will not be outdone in generosity, that He begins to give it special helps, that He begins to take over a greater part of the work of the soul's advancement, and shares with it His own strength. Such a soul will find itself becoming more and more united to God in thought, in outlook, and in action, and its prayer will develop accordingly.

Now, there is one error which is a great obstacle to this develop- ment and must, therefore, be avoided, though it must be admitted that this erroneous view finds some support in the works of certain authors who reacted too strongly against the errors of their own time. As we saw, some think that there is no different state of prayer after ordinary meditation in its strict sense save the extraordinary phenomena that are associated in many minds with the heights of sanctity. This is a serious error, and all that has been written here about the development of prayer along the lines of human friend- ship should help the reader to avoid it and to see that, on the con- trary, prayer should be capable of infinite degrees of growth, and may reasonably be expected to lead to such a complete union of heart and soul with God that it should become contemplation. It must not be thought that the extraordinary ecstasies and visions that we read of in the lives of some saints are an essential part either of sanctity or of the higher states of contemplation. Far from it; not only are they no part of true prayer—for there are some who went to the top of the ladder of prayer without showing any of these effects—but they are even sometimes a manifestation of the lack of complete perfection in the state of prayer of that soul, and may be due to human weakness; though, of course, they may also be the direct work of God, designed to carry out His own special plans in regard to a particular soul. In practice, anyhow, they lie outside the essential path of prayer, which leads one deeper and deeper into the depths of one's own soul, there to find one's self completely united to God.

However late it be when a soul sees the full possibilities of the spiritual life or finds the right way of prayer, it is of great importance that the resolve to advance to close union with God be not overcome by the fear that now it is too late. Even though the past has been stained by sin, or time has been wasted through mistaken direction or an unsuitable way of praying, there can be nothing—absolutely nothing of any sort whatsoever—in the past that can be an insuperable obstacle to holiness, if we but turn our hearts to God. He is our Saviour, that is His Name. He became man to save us from our sins, and surely He will save us from our mistakes! "To them that love God, all things work together unto good," writes St. Paul, and that includes even our sins. God has infinite power and infinite mercy; He can utilise all our past and turn it to good account. No matter how late the hour, or how great the obstacles, we must turn to God with unlimited confidence. In fact, since all the glory is to be His, there will always be some apparently insuperable difficulty or weakness on our part. Nevertheless, "all things are possible to him that believeth"; no matter what is lacking to us, be it time or merit, "our sufficiency is from God."

CHAPTER TWENTY-ONE

CONCLUSION

So many readers will probably feel that much of what has been written in the later chapters has no practical reference to themselves, that one cannot help quoting St. John of the Cross, who is the authority *par excellence* on this subject. In his book, *The Living Flame of Love,* when treating of the development of the prayer of meditation, he writes:

> The state of beginners . . . is one of meditation and of acts of reflection. It is necessary to furnish the soul in this state with matter for meditation, that it may make reflections and interior acts, and avail itself of the sensible spiritual heat and fervour, for this is necessary in order to accustom the senses and desires to good things, that, being satisfied by the sweetness thereof, they may be detached from the world. When this is in some degree effected, God begins at once to introduce the soul into the state of contemplation, *and that very quickly, especially in the case of religious,* (italics are ours) because these, having renounced the world, quickly fashion their senses and desires according to God; they have, therefore, to pass at once from meditation to contemplation. This passage, then, takes place when the discursive acts and meditation fail, when sensible sweetness and first fervours cease, when the soul cannot make reflections as before, nor find any sensible comfort, but is fallen into aridity, because the chief matter is changed into the spirit, and the spirit is not cognisable by sense. As all the natural operations of the soul, which are within its control, depend on the senses only, it follows

that God is now working in a special manner in this state, that it is He that infuses and teaches, that the soul is the recipient on which He bestows spiritual blessings by contemplation, the knowledge and the love of Himself together; that is, He gives it loving knowledge without the instrumentality of its discursive acts, because it is no longer able to form them as before.

At this time, then, the direction of the soul must be wholly different from what it was at first. If formerly it was supplied with matter for meditation and it did meditate, now that matter must be withheld and meditation must cease, because, as I have said, it cannot meditate, do what it will, and distractions are the result. If before it looked for fervour and sweetness and found them, let it look for them no more nor desire them; and if it attempt to seek them, not only will it not find them, but it will meet with aridity, because it turns away from the peaceful and tranquil good secretly bestowed upon it, when it attempts to fall back on the operations of sense. In this way it loses the latter without gaining the former, because the senses have ceased to be the channel of spiritual good.

The primary purpose in quoting this long passage is to draw attention to the words in which the Saint indicates for us the fundamental disposition for the passage to contemplation, namely: that one has fashioned one's senses and desires according to God, which disposition, with its result, he expects to find quickly reached in the case of religious. But the whole passage has been quoted because it sums up in pregnant language, weighted with all the authority of the Church's Doctor of Prayer, all that these pages have been trying to say. The holy doctor's opinion of the effect that may be naturally expected from life in the religious state, both as to formation in virtue and advance in prayer, will be found to be quite similar to the hopes held out by St. Teresa in her writings. The essence of the religious state has not changed since their time; it is a state of tending to perfection. Now, it is impossible to tend properly and completely to perfection without leading an interior life. We may go further and say that without an interior life it is impossible for a priest or a religious to live an exterior life that is not ruined by sterility, supernatural uselessness, and inefficacy.

If there be anything wrong with our priests and religious of today—if there be any failure even on the part of the laity to live up to the faith that they undoubtedly possess—if our resistance to the infiltration of a pagan civilisation, of pagan manners, and of pagan principles into our minds and hearts, into our public and our private life, is not as vigorous, as sturdy, as resourceful, as it should be—the cause is surely to be found in the lack of an interior life, and, fundamentally, in the lack of such a life in its proper measure among priests and religious. With the best will in the world, it is not easy to be assured that all is as it should be. There are not wanting voices—competent voices—crying out in warning; there are not lacking signs—unmistakeable signs—giving them support; it is even said that supernatural admonitions are not unheard of, all deploring the lack of due fervour and interior life in religion. It is not for us to attempt to pass judgment upon the state of affairs. But it is for each of us to examine his own condition, and see whether it is in harmony with the wonderful spiritual equipment that God has given each one of us in Baptism. For God Himself has come to live in our souls, to be our Guide, our Strength, our Life, and our Love.

The real root of the trouble is that we do not realise, nor have we a lively practical faith in, the effects of Baptism and the possibilities of the Christian life. We do not realise that the Christian life is the life of Christ lived by Christ in us, not merely our own paltry existence dragged out in lonely weakness. We do not estimate the interior life at its proper worth nor give it its due place in our scale of values. For many of us, the spiritual life, and especially the religious life, is a life of external practices and works, in which greatness and success is measured in much the same way as in any other walk of life. As a result, our spiritual programme is closely and narrowly limited—limited by a feeling that when all is said and done, our progress will depend upon our own selves, upon our own strength of character, our own will-power, our own resources; and knowing these to be so poor, we cannot help feeling that such things as progress in holiness and advance in prayer are not for us.

This, of course, is one of those half-truths that are the greatest of all errors. It is true that God has told us that without Him we can do nothing, but has His Holy Spirit not also written for our consolation that we can do all things in Him who strengthens us? It is true that the world is in us and is dragging us down to its own level, but have we not heard Our Lord's assurance that He has overcome the world? Now, is there any closer union of strength than that of

Baptism—where the Spirit of God so unites Himself to the soul as
to make it a living member of the Body of the Son of God—where
God divinises the soul in its strength and in its possibilities? If the
Sacraments effect what they signify—and that is the official formula for their action—what conclusion must be drawn from the fact
that in the Sacrament of the Blessed Eucharist the Body and Blood
of Christ is given to us for our *food?*—what limit may we set to the
strength or to the possibilities of a soul which is nourished by the living Flesh of God Himself? The wonder is not that a priest or a religious should be expected to aspire to high perfection and to the
graces of prayer, but rather that any priest or religious, or even any
Catholic, should fail not only to aim at them, but even, as a general rule, to attain them!

Perhaps this failure to realise the "talents" that they are leaving
buried in their souls is the reason why so many religious take such a
distorted view of their religious life. For many, the day's work consists of some special duty—teaching or preaching or nursing or
study, for example—as its principal and essential part, with a number of devotional exercises inserted as a sort of accidental colour-
ing, a necessary concession to one's state of life, but for all that,
something by no means of first-rate importance—something which
is often a considerable handicap to the main task and at times rather
a nuisance! As for the interior life—well, that is a matter, they say,
of a special vocation, which has nothing to do with the ordinary
religious. Here we have a complete reversal of the true scale of values coupled with a capital error as to the nature of the primary and
essential purpose of the religious state, which—no matter what may
be the nature or particular purpose of a particular congregation—
is *always* the sanctification of the individual members, to which
everything else must, in a general way, be subordinated.

To these two errors one can trace most of the surprise that many
readers will feel on seeing the above words of St. John of the Cross
applied to modern religious; in fact, much of what has been written
in this book will appear to many as far-fetched and unpractical—as
a mistaken application to the religious life in general, of what, they
say, is really peculiar to the contemplative life. This view is really a
result of the erroneous opinions which have just been pointed out.
The essential nature of the Christian life and of the religious state
have not changed one whit; and all conclusions based on those

natures are as valid now as they were in all ages of the Church. Holiness is still a primary duty, and a practical possibility. Our Lord's exhortation to be perfect as the Father in Heaven is perfect is still just as insistent and just as feasible as it was the day He uttered it.

Every single Christian soul can say:

> During every moment of His life Jesus thought of *me*, and loved *me*; in all His sufferings He had *my* needs in His mind, and in His view; in all His joys, His Heart was set on sharing these joys with *me*; in all His labours, in all His teaching, He never ceased to have *my* holiness in view; one of His greatest tortures was His longing for *my* happiness and *my* love; He knew that He had done and suffered more than a hundred times enough to make me holy, to make me a saint. He saw clearly that the only obstacle to the achievement of His cherished purpose for me was my own refusal to trust Him, to believe in Him, to cast all my cares upon Him—to take Him at His word, and to submit to His easy yoke and to the light burden which He had specially planned for me; for He, seeing my poverty, had, as it were, lived my life for me with His own perfection, and was longing for the day when I would make my own the result of His labour and suffering, by doing what He asked me to do.

All this is no exaggeration: Jesus has merited everything for us, even the power to make His merits our own. He only needs our good-will and humility to make us enter into the fruits of His labours. Nor need we think that Jesus loses sight of each of us in the enormous number of the faithful: He is God, and has all God's infinity. His intense love for each one is not a whit the less because of His glowing love for all men. In fact, we get a truer picture of the Heart of Jesus by remembering that He loved *me*, and delivered Himself for *me*, than by considering ourselves as one of the millions sharing His heart.

Every act of Christ's life was one of intense longing and passionate love for me. Nor has that love lessened in His life in the Sacrament of the Altar. Still more can I be sure that it is no less in His life in my soul. In that awful moment in the Garden, in the depths of what in anyone else would be called despair, when He uttered that cry of bitterest agony, of which the Psalmist speaks in the words: "What is the use of My Blood?"—it was from my failure to correspond with His grace that He was suffering; it was my sins, my refusal to trust Him, my rejection of His pleading, my disbelief of His love, my distrust of His power and of His plans, my hardheartedness and my selfishness, my self-sufficiency and my sloth, that were in His mind and that caused Him to pour out the sweat of His precious Blood. He still implores us to let His work bear fruit in our lives, to set some value on His Precious Blood, to have some trust, some faith in His power and in His love.

Truly, only too truly, can He still say to us: " Oh! ye of little faith: why do you doubt?" The charity of Christ urgeth us; the love of Him Who first loved us cries out to us; let us stir up the grace, the faith, the hope, the love that is in us by the Sacraments of water, of oil, and of the Body and Blood of God. Let us think of what our daily Food is, and see what our strength and our life should be. Let us cease saying that these things are not for me, and remember that it is no longer I who live, but Christ Who liveth in me. Let us realise that our strength is Christ's strength, that our hopes and our possibilities are Christ's possibilities, that our needs are Christ's needs, that our merits are Christ's merits, that our spirit is Christ's Spirit—the Paraclete, the " Strengthener," the Spirit of God—and we shall renew our courage and our earnestness, and filled with fresh hope and complete confidence in the word of God, remembering that we are the Body of Christ, we shall launch out again into the deep, where we have long been labouring without success, now determined to seek with confidence for that perfection which the Heart of Jesus longs to find in us, to produce in us, and with us.

In particular, let each soul renew his hope and his intention of persevering in prayer. First, he must resolve with determination, never under any circumstances to give up his attempt to progress in prayer. Let him take up prayer as he should take up the whole of the spiritual life, as a quest for Jesus, a striving for close union with Jesus. Let him meditate as long as is necessary—during spiritual reading, if needs be—but let him proceed to pray to Our Lord in his own words as soon as he can and as often as he can. Let him not be afraid to talk to God without words whenever he can, and so all the time he is coming nearer to Jesus. Let him throughout the day make frequent aspirations to Jesus; they should not be long, they need not be verbal; a sigh or a smile of the heart is sufficient. Let him seek Jesus in all things; let him unite himself to Jesus by doing what pleases Him—by doing the will of God. That is the way to lay hold of Jesus. When the time comes, when he can feel Jesus near, let him make full use of it; but he must not be so attached to this sensible presence of Jesus as to refuse to let Him go when the Master decides it is expedient for the soul that He should deprive it of His sensible presence and send it another Comforter.

If all power of prayer seems to be lost, if the time of prayer becomes a period of distraction and aridity, let him not lose courage, nor change his resolution. His prayer then is made by submitting to the will of God as completely and as generously as he can. He need not be afraid to make use of any available expedient to help him to fight distractions. Many get great help by using a book, but this must not be done in such a way as to turn prayer into spiritual reading; one must stop frequently and turn one's heart to God, and listen to see if He has not something to say to him. Perseverance under this heavy trial has a great reward, and touches the heart of God. The soul should try to be ready to accept any suffering that God sends him, for union with Jesus is sealed in the fellowship of His sufferings and by our patient endurance we are made partakers of the Passion of Christ. But our chief aim must be humility. The Kingdom of God is already within us, but we make it our own by our poverty of spirit. This is our title to union with God, and it is the first principle of the spiritual life that Our Lord taught in public. The soul, then, must never, never trust in itself, and, above all, it must never, never, under any circumstances, cease to trust Jesus absolutely; God became man to save sinners, to give life to those who are dead in sin, to give strength to the weak and weary, to give Himself to the humble, to the poor in spirit. Let us take Him at His word, let us take Him at His Name, let us submit ourselves to Him in obedient humility and loving confidence, let us say to Him with Mary: " Be it done by me, be it done to me, according to Thy word," and then we shall be filled with Christ, through Whom and with Whom and in Whom, in the unity of the Holy Spirit, is all the glory of God.

Appendix

There seem to be two different views of the purpose of the exercise known as meditation, running through the literature of the subject. Sometimes its reflective nature is stressed, and it is considered to be a means of building up an idea of God, of His Son's human life, of supernatural truths and of forming convictions, which will be the main-spring of our spiritual life. At other times, the function of reflections is subordinated to the production of affections, and stress is laid upon the acts which are to be made. One might say that one view sees it as a work of the head, while the other regards it as a work of the heart. That contrast, however, would be too sharp. Even though reflections, theoretically speaking, are quite distinct from the affections, yet, in practice, they are not so easily separated. In practice, one cannot think of such subjects without being moved towards the production of some sort of affection, even though this be quite unconscious; nor can one talk to Our Lord without in some way thinking about Him. Still there is, perhaps, a difference of stress between the two views, and this is why some would prefer to be less definite about the setting aside of considerations when affections begin to come, than we have been in chapters 3 and 4.

No one can question the value of systematic reflection for the formation of the spiritual life, but there are many souls who find such difficulty in persevering in it, that they are in danger of giving up the exercise, without providing any substitute for it. To lessen that danger we have stressed the affective aspect of mental prayer, and at the same time, insisted on the importance of spiritual reading. These two recommendations must be taken together; they are both indispensable parts of the one plan of reversing the tendency to compression, and of distributing over different parts of the day the exercises that are sometimes grouped together under the name of meditation. It should also be noted that we have insisted, firstly, that meditation, in the sense of that informal and often spontaneous thinking about spiritual things during the course of the day, should never be given up; and secondly, that a soul must be ready to return to the use of formal considerations when that is possible at the time of prayer, if and whenever the facility for the formation of acts ceases. This latter point applies, not only to one particular hour of prayer, but also to a whole period of one's spiritual life. It is only on such conditions that one can safely urge concentration upon the affective aspect of mental prayer.

In our view, both mental prayer and spiritual reading (or their equivalents) are normally essential for a healthy spiritual life. We look to spiritual reading, and the consequent informal reflection to which it leads, for the formation of those ideas and convictions that are sought by systematic meditation.

A time may come when neither consideration or affections are possible at prayer, and aridity and distractions are such that one feels the need of some help. It is consoling to remember that St. Teresa, who had advanced fairly far in the ways of prayer during the first years of her religious life, afterwards found herself unable to pray without a book, for more than fourteen years. A suitable book, then, can be a great help to souls in such circumstances. They should, however, be careful not to pass the whole time of prayer in mere reading, but should frequently pause, either to make some attempt at affections of some sort, with or without words, or at least to permit the development of any affection, however imperceptible, that may have arisen from the reading. It sometimes happens that the only way to keep distractions in check is to keep a book open and proceed in this fashion. The best type of book is one which contains sufficient acts, but their style and content must be in harmony with the soul's outlook; whatever is not suitable should be passed over. Even if one pauses to murmur only the Name of Jesus or that of His Blessed Mother, one may be quite satisfied with such attempts at prayer.

Dom M. Eugene Boylan, O.C.R., was an Irish-born Trappist monk and writer who was born in 1904 and died in 1964. Ordained a priest in 1937, he began writing on spiritual topics, and in the 1940s he published two books, *This Tremendous Lover* and *Difficulties in Mental Prayer*, which became international bestsellers and were translated into many languages. In the late 1950s he undertook an extensive lecture tour of the United States ("This is the best retreat we ever had at Gethsemani," commented Thomas Merton after Boylan's visit there), and in 1962 he was elected the fourth abbot of Mount St. Joseph Abbey in Roscrea, Ireland. Two years later he died in an automobile accident.